This book is dedicated to all the amazing people that we met on this journey from Europe and throughout the countries of the Middle East and Asia. This is as much their story as it is mine because it is they who give the account much of its colour. We were shown amazing kindness from the majority of people we met, regardless of their religious faith or circumstances. They helped me to see that we are indeed one human family.

Acknowledgements

I am deeply grateful to David Chanter who has been a wonderful support in the writing of this book and without whom I would never have embarked on this exciting overland journey.

Many thanks go to those who supported me in various ways including my friends: Lena Axelsson, Elizabeth Barber, Sophie Brookes, Hazel Carey, Clare Walters and Barbara Wheeler. I would particularly like to thank Carrie Foggitt for her help and encouragement throughout the editorial process and for writing the generous-hearted foreword.

Special thanks also go to David's friend Jeremy Taylor for his comments, to my friend Derek Wheeler MBE for proof reading the first printed edition and to James Chanter who improved the quality of the aged photos and drew the map.

I am also grateful to Wikipedia for all the times I was able to check my facts and to Pauline Tebbutt and Simon Potter at Fast-Print Publishing for their help.

My thanks also go to anyone who encouraged me to write this account, including my family: daughters Lisa Pitman and Tamsin Alsbury, their husbands John and Simon, my nephew Steve Andrews and his partner Zoe Chiverton, my brother Richard Andrews and cousin Sarah Matthews; my godchildren Natasha and Tim Smith; my friends: Alison Alsbury, Sam Attenborough, Angiras Auro, Irene Caminiti, Roisin Carlton, Susie Castay, Anna Clifford, Vivian Choi, Manisha Dahad, Jas Dale, Julie Daly, Tina Deards, Des and Catherine Dornan, Susanne Forster, Frances Hurst, Ľudmila Krnáčová, Anthony Leonard, Sue Lines, the

Matnam family, Christine and Iver Miskelly, Nathalie Montille, Liz and Bryan Pitman, Christine and George Reason, Sarah Reason and Nicole Rubio.

Contents

INNOCENTS ABROAD:
An Overland Trip Through A World That No Longer Exists

Foreword

O ne grey day in 1977 I recall entering an outwardly drab north London house, being taken upstairs to the first floor flat and entering a small living room dominated by a huge indoor garden of large and gracious plants set among pools of water. There was talk of a vague plan to support some of the weight of soil and water from the ceiling above. Luckily, although that didn't happen, the hazards predicted by the more fearful among us did not come about.

This is my memory of my first visit to Carol at home. At that time she was training in social work; I was working in housing. She was thinking about starting a family and I was preparing to travel overland which was something she had done ten years earlier.

While we were both working with people whose lives had brought considerable challenges and deprivation, my focus was very much on social and material justice. Carol's focus, while compassionate, seemed to me a little unpredictable and unexpected. For example, I was shocked at first when I mentioned the need to march against nuclear weapons and Carol simply said it was not her way.

From the first meeting, I noticed Carol's unusual reaction to challenges, events, statements and situations around her. Whereas others might react with fear, defensiveness or pride, Carol's reactions were usually open and interested. While most of my friends would be sympathetically outraged by my descriptions of personal or social wrongs and pain, she offered curiosity and encouragement to find a new approach. It took me a while to understand Carol's philosophy of life, that if we first take responsibility for our own growth rather than reacting to the wrongs around us, what we then contribute to our world brings about positive change.

As Carol has worked with and learned from the challenges that her life has brought her over the 40 years that I have known her, she has been an inspiration and guide as well as a close friend and mentor to me and to my family and indeed to many others. Through times of darkness, turbulence and major challenges, her steady wisdom has always been there, uplifting and encouraging me to move forward to new perspectives and to find my way to greater autonomy and inner health.

It's now a cliché to say that 'life is a journey'. However, Carol is the person who showed me that this is truly so; that what matters is not what happens or what we see per se, but rather how we live with and respond to life's offerings; that the challenges we face are the grist to the mill of our growth as a person. I learned how we all, whether we know it or not, are provided with the challenges that help us do this. I have even come to accept her wisdom, that each difficult situation brings a gift: it is not usually seen at the time, but if we look back over our life to those challenges, we realise what qualities and skills we developed as a result.

In reading this journal of an overland trip, you will find yourself reading about places that have now changed beyond recognition and people who may no longer live there or even be alive. You will also find that you might be learning how to travel well; perhaps even about travelling through life.

Carrie Smith

Introduction

A part from a brief explanation of how we met, this account spans a period from the beginning of August 1969 to the end of June 1970. I made this trip with David, my husband at the time. We left England to go on what we intended to be a short package holiday on the island of Ibiza but ended up doing the so-called hippie trip to Kathmandu in Nepal and then on to what was then known as Ceylon; now as Sri Lanka. This particular journey took place at a very specific time and was unique: it would not be possible to come even close to repeating it. Not only was it unplanned, on impulse and with no preconceptions, but also it was rare and risky to undertake such a journey at that time with so little knowledge and information available and the impossibility of staying in touch with our families.

I believe it is true to say that the classic hippie trail, which started in the late 1960s, came to an end in 1979 with the Islamic revolution in Iran and the establishment of the world's first Islamic state, and with the Russian invasion of Afghanistan. Civil war in Lebanon and tensions in other areas also grew at that time.

This is not a travel guide, but rather an account taken from my journal in Ibiza and the diaries we both kept which charted the experiences we had each day from when we left Ibiza. At the time, I was writing purely for myself to look back on in later years. David took the slides and in that pre-digital age, film was expensive and difficult to come by, so he had to choose carefully which pictures to take.

I made the decision to start writing this account in 2012 partly for our families and descendants because I was approaching 70. However, what really impelled me to write it was that I found myself thinking about this trip every time I heard the news about the escalation of conflict in the Arab world known as the Arab Spring. It had begun mainly because the people wanted democratic and economic reform. Syria in particular was on my mind. We had arrived there about forty one years before the unrest which began on 13th March 2011. This had started as largely peaceful protests against President Bashar al-Assad and developed into a full-scale civil war with government forces and rebel groups engaged in violent battles across the country. Now in 2015, other nations and factions are involving themselves politically, logistically and militarily on both sides.

Our reason for making this trip was that we were intrigued to know what life was like for people in the Middle East and Asia at that time. It is particularly interesting in the light of what is happening now to let others know what the people we met were saying then. I have not repeated their views in order to make any personal, political or religious points. I know that their opinions were subjective as all opinions are, but for the most part, I felt that the views that people shared with us were held with deep conviction. When I listened to them pouring out their hearts to us I felt that in some way I was there to bear witness to them.

As I was writing this account and listening daily to the horrors taking place in Syria, I found myself thinking often of the people we met. With so many thousands of people now dead, I know that the same fate could also have befallen them. I am also mindful of the fact that some of the sites and beautiful buildings that we saw in Syria have been destroyed or damaged, such as the wonderful Umayyad Mosque in Damascus. I am also aware that huge destruction has taken place in Afghanistan since we were there.

Another reason for writing this account now is for others to be able to compare our present world with one that no longer exists. This journey took place when life was very different both in the UK and other parts of the western world and also in the countries we visited. We didn't have computers with access to all that we wanted to know, nor was there instant twenty four hour news or travel guides. There were no mobiles so communication with others was not the immediate and easy matter that it is now. England was much less multicultural then so we were not familiar with the customs, religions, music, dress or food of others. It is hard to imagine what a completely different experience of life we had in those days but to do so would give you some idea of how this journey was for us and the courage needed. Few of us were aware of what was going on in different parts of the world. In many ways, David and I represented both the vision and the naivety of the time.

It was actually a very exciting time, especially for many of us who were young in Britain, Europe and the USA. For others no doubt it was a disturbing time as change so often is. There was much political unrest. The fact that the Americans were involved in the Vietnam war and were enlisting their young men to fight was one of the factors promoting rebellion against the status quo. One of their ways to escape this draft was to leave the country, either to travel or to emigrate.

Just as the War in Vietnam was having a significant impact on American society, so the student riots in Paris in May 1968 were impacting French society. They were also affecting other countries in Europe and further afield such as in the student campuses in Japan and Mexico. The events in Paris took place just after the first serious student uprising in the United States. Parisian students clashed with police and much of the work force joined in, even though it was a time of prosperity for the French. Consequently, Charles de Gaulle lost his presidency. The ramifications were not just political: there were far reaching changes to every aspect of society. To many of us, it seemed that a new world order, innocent of conspiracy theory, was taking shape.[1]

---

[1] www.histclo.com/country/fran/co-fran1968.html. Author: Dennis Weidner

In fact, it seemed that the whole world was restless. Of the other popular movements taking place that spring, one of the most publicised in England was the Prague Spring. This was a period of political liberalisation in Czechoslovakia during the era of its domination by the Soviet Union after the Second World War.

Given that I had grown up with the fear that Russia would invade England, it was amazing to me that the Czechoslovakian Communist leader Alexander Dubcek was doing what he could to bring more personal and political freedom to his country. However, this period was to last for only four months. I remember being very upset to see pictures on the television news of the Warsaw Pact troops invading Prague on 20th August 1968 and the great tanks rolling into the streets confronting the people. Apparently, more than a hundred were killed and Dubcek and the other Communist leaders were arrested and taken to Moscow.[2]

Another exciting manifestation of this restlessness and pioneering spirit could be seen in the exploration of space and the desire for man to reach the moon. The race had been carried out between the USA and the USSR, and on 21st July 1969, the USA succeeded in landing Apollo 11 for the first human to step onto the moon. As the mission commander Neil Armstrong set foot on the moon's surface he uttered the immortal words, 'One small step for man, one giant leap for mankind.' The phrase 'the sky's the limit' seemed to be as tangible as it was symbolic.

The fact is that many of us were finding a voice for the first time and feeling that those of us with vision could really make a difference. We could feel that society was changing in a radical way: there was a fundamental dissatisfaction with the materialistic values of the West and a feeling in some of us that the ideas of the East could balance this out in some way and give more emphasis to the values of love, compassion, kindness and peace than to acquisition, conflict and war. All this went hand in hand with a

---

[2] http://news.bbc.co.uk/1/hi/world/europe/155500.stm

renaissance of thinking and creativity which liberalised music, cinema, dance, education, gender, sex and ways of dressing.

I think that the change at this time was impelled partly by the need for more of what might be called feminine values to come into being to balance the predominantly masculine ones, with more weight given to feelings and self-awareness. This same impulsion took a different form in the hippie movement from the form it took in feminism which had more to do with equality of gender, but that is a whole subject in itself.

Some younger men and women of working age dropped out of the work scene completely. Many used psychedelic drugs and / or marijuana to further the expansion of their consciousness and loosen up their adherence to the previous rigid norms of society. Taking what was known as the hippie trip overland was also a way of expanding consciousness, most people travelling from country to country by local transport. Some were inspired by the Beatles trip to Rishikesh in India in 1968 where they studied Transcendental Meditation. However, I think it is probably true to say that many of these travellers were going as much to find a way of getting hold of drugs cheaply as to find out what else the world had to offer beside the nine to five work imperative.

David and I were both spiritual in our own different ways but we were never truly hippies. At the time, David was an architectural technician and I was a teacher. We weren't interested in drugs or in dropping out of the work scene for any length of time. What interested us was the counter culture and the changes that were taking place in the West and in the rest of the world. We were reading underground literature such as the 'International Times' newspaper, launched in 1966 and later known as 'IT'. We wanted to explore more of the world and felt the need to break away from the restrictions of the past, to open up to new ways of looking at the world.

David was primarily interested in the British colonial and indigenous architecture and in the process of travel. He thought of travel as opening a new book and experiencing it page by page. He found it creative to travel in that way and to rely on systems and people to provide a means of support for living and surviving on the road. My interest, apart from the scenery and customs, was primarily in people and their thinking as this account shows. We set off a few weeks after the Apollo landing.

The hippie trail lasted a little more than 10 years. David and I were among the first of these travellers but thousands followed, especially once the first Lonely Planet Guide was produced by Tony Wheeler in 1973.

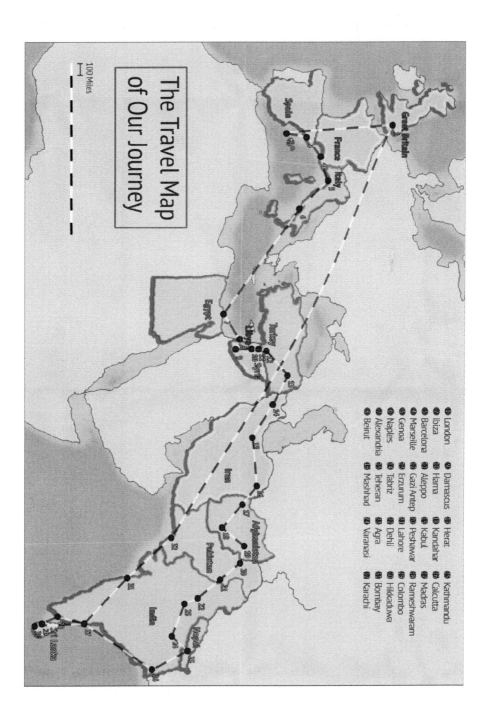

The Travel Map
of Our Journey

100 Miles

① London
② Ibiza
③ Barcelona
④ Marseille
⑤ Genoa
⑥ Naples
⑦ Alexandria
⑧ Beirut

❾ Damascus
❿ Hama
⓫ Aleppo
⓬ Gazi Antep
⓭ Erzurum
⓮ Tabriz
⓯ Teheran
⓰ Mashhad

⓱ Herat
⓲ Kandahar
⓳ Kabul
⓴ Peshawar
㉑ Lahore
㉒ Dehli
㉓ Agra
㉔ Varanasi

㉕ Kathmandu
㉖ Calcutta
㉗ Madras
㉘ Rameshwaram
㉙ Colombo
㉚ Hikkaduwa
㉛ Bombay
㉜ Karachi

Carol And David As They Were On Their Travels

David's 1969 passport photo

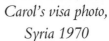

Carol's visa photo, Syria 1970

The Door Opens

When a knock at the door comes unexpectedly, it can be an interruption, a surprise and sometimes an opportunity, the scope of which could never be guessed. When a young man with the face of an angel knocks on a young woman's door, I guess she should be ready for something out of the ordinary. And so it proved to be for me in 1965. David had simply come from next door to paint my room for the landlady, but he was to become a good friend, then my husband and about five years later, to lead me into an adventure of a lifetime.

After I had worked for four years as a teacher, and David for longer as an architectural technician, he decided to become fully qualified as an architect. This would entail seven years of training. As we had the summer ahead of us before his course started, we decided to have a two week package holiday in Ibiza. It was 1969: a year of astounding events round the world but we had no inkling that this holiday was to open the door to a completely different world for us too. It intrigues me how people's futures often seem to rest on apparently random choices made in a moment. Such is the mystery of serendipity.

On the final day of our holiday in Ibiza we were having breakfast outside on the patio at our hotel in San Antonio, our cases packed ready to catch the flight back to England. Suddenly, David suggested that we stay on in Ibiza and see if we could get work. We had little time to consider the consequences of such a decision as we needed to be at the airport within the hour. However, we both felt ready for something out of the ordinary to expand our lives. As we watched our plane leaving for England from the comfort of our hotel, disbelief wrestled with excitement.

Carol Carlton

Ibiza

We had made no plans to stay in Ibiza but here we were, luxuriating in our extra time in the hotel knowing that soon we would have to leave. We stayed there for as long as the hotel allowed us to that day, then faced the practical considerations for our continued stay. We decided to take our luggage and catch a bus to Ibiza town, the hub of Ibiza Island. We found a wooden seat in the Square and made the decision to spend the night there until the town came to life the following morning. We then planned to go into one of the bars to meet the locals and see if we could find work.

The bars opened very early for the fishermen who had just been working overnight, and locals also came in for a strong coffee before going to work. No more than a few minutes had passed before we met a woman called Maggie who was an architect, and we were amazed when she offered David a job.

Her partner Erica happened to own an antique shop and a school for teaching English to the islanders, other Spaniards and foreigners. Maggie thought that she would be delighted to have me as a teacher there and indeed that proved to be the case. We found an apartment quite easily too, seven floors up in a block of flats in Figuaretes which was on the coast overlooking the sea and only a one mile walk away. So within the first day we were set up for six months of Ibiza Island living and working and an escape from the English winter.

We found it a fascinating experience with the challenges as interesting and enjoyable as the obvious delights of being in a beautiful, sunny and relaxed island with beaches in every direction. Although David and I had always been very interested in the counter culture of the 60s, our time in Ibiza was only a semi drop-out experience on our parts as we were as much part of the capitalistic world of work and earning as we were of the alternative scenes there. We were to discover that it was a place where people who hadn't felt welcome or safe in other parts of the world had come to settle. There were many gays, in those days known by the unfortunate title of 'queers'; artists, writers and people who for whatever reason wanted to leave their own country.

It was also a magnet for the draft dodgers from the USA who were escaping being drafted into the military to fight in the Vietnam War. By this time, opposition to the war in the USA was proving divisive and politically controversial. As U.S. troop strength in Vietnam increased, more young men sought to avoid the draft: some evaded the draft and some deserted, though we never asked those we met which they were. The majority had fled to Canada and many went to Sweden, France, and the United Kingdom. Some made it to Kathmandu in Nepal which was also becoming a major destination for many hippies and other young travellers.

Most of the 'ex-pats' in Ibiza seemed to be involved in drinking excessive amounts of alcohol, which was inexpensive, and the Americans and hippies in smoking a lot of pot. We managed to remain light in our intake of both and I didn't enjoy the effect on me of pot smoking at all, finding it made me feel lonely and isolated. People who smoked dope seemed to become very uncommunicative except in a superficial way. We could go to a party that mainly consisted of everyone sitting in a circle on the floor at the edge of the room while the spliff was passed round to each person. With each turn, they became increasingly quiet and self-involved as they considered how pure the cannabis was and the effects on their experience.

We didn't get to know local people that well. The Ibicencos we met rarely spoke any English, and Spaniards generally still felt under surveillance under Franco's regime. We occasionally met a local painter called Manolo but one of our more interesting friendships was with a German woman called Anna Wachsman who had settled in the countryside of Ibiza many years ago. She had been married to the well-known German architect Konrad Wachsman who had made his name as part of the Chicago set.

She was a wonderful source of knowledge and gossip on the people we met while we were in Ibiza. Unfortunately, her health was not good and she needed to go into a hospital in London for two weeks but she wouldn't say what was wrong with her. She asked us if we would look after her finca, - the name of the local organic-looking farmsteads of the countryside. She also had plants that needed to be watered and a large tom cat. We were only too happy to do all of this. I loved cats and it was wonderful to wake up in the heart of the countryside and have access to the comforts of a home and her wonderful library of novels.

Once ensconced in her home I started to devour some of the novels of authors that I hadn't previously encountered such as Saul Bellow, Isaac Bashevis Singer and Gore Vidal.

She had told us on no account to let her friend into the house because this friend kept chickens and she would bring fleas. Unfortunately, the said friend arrived in the house before we could stop her and afterwards we had a tricky time wrestling with our bedding, trying to locate and destroy all the fleas she'd left in her wake. This particular species seemed to be bigger than any we had ever met before and capable of some serious, poison-filled biting.

When Anna returned, we were quite sad to leave her lovely home. When we next saw her, she told me she was very cross with me. I was puzzled and couldn't think what I had done. She told me that I had ruined her cat for her! When she had left for England, apparently he had been a fiercely independent tom, but on her return, she found him wanting to be cuddled on her lap all the time. Yes, it was true: I had indeed tamed him!

One day, Maggie invited us to a party at the home that she had designed for herself in Ibiza town. David and I found ourselves to be the only heterosexual couple there. It was definitely a time of widening our concept of normality and of experiencing life as the ones who were in the minority which was interesting and quite humbling.

View of Ibiza town.

Something else happened at the party that night which was a very unpleasant experience for me. Before we even set foot inside her home I found myself unconsciously walking past the door even though I had been there many times before. David called me back and we found that we were the only ones there apart from Maggie. She took me aside and told me in serious tones that I was going to be very ill. She said she could see it in my eyes and had seen the same look in a friend of hers who had become very ill. I was angry with her but also terrified and perhaps some part of me recognised the truth of it. In fact, not long after this, something happened which was a warning of this, though I had no idea at the time as it simply felt like a special and rather spiritual experience.

During my time in Ibiza, it seems that I was thoroughly involved in reflecting on the truths of Christian Science, (not to be confused with Scientology) which was something that I had studied since the age of six. I was involved in a correspondence with Peggy Brook, one of the leading lights in non-church Christian Science, about the significance of my experience in Ibiza. It seemed that I thought of Ibiza as a spiritual wilderness where people came to find their true identity: that being on a small island gave people the chance to experience life cut off from their usual frames of reference. I haven't changed my mind about this but reading my comments, I can see that I was doing too much thinking and wrestling with spiritual concepts that did not fit easily with my experience.

On this occasion, what I experienced came in the form of my spending the whole of one night in a bright light unable to sleep. My head was humming, I felt super-conscious and in a state of bliss. There is perhaps a connection between what I experienced and shamanism: that journey into the 'other side' but it was dangerous for me because I was not in any way sufficiently grounded or connected to the feelings in my body. What I understood as spiritual truths was not at all integrated into my actual experience of myself and my life. I did not realise this at the time of course but Maggie's prediction did come true soon after I returned to England and forced me to understand why this was and how to integrate my spiritual with my physical life. In fact, it was to become my main purpose in life.

Meanwhile, we were having a lovely life-style, eating good, healthy food, meeting all kinds of people, and particularly enjoying the company of John whose parents were English but who had emigrated to Australia when he was a young boy. We had actually first met John when we lived in Devon though I don't remember the circumstances of it. My main memory of him then was that he was very partial to the local strong cider called scrumpy. Several hours into a party that we had all been invited to, we heard loud bangs at the door competing with the music. On opening the door we discovered a policeman holding the inebriated John up, asking if this young man belonged to us! We told him he did and the tolerant policeman handed him over to us with a smile. It was powerful stuff that scrumpy.

We also sometimes visited another friend with him in Ibiza, an art dealer called Vicki who had bought a beautiful finca. The domestic architecture of Ibiza was of the North African Moorish style with simple white walls and flat roofs. Our friend's finca was quite large in Ibizan terms and had the atmosphere of a simple chapel inside. We spent many an evening there in the candlelight, sharing a couple of bottles of red wine and having interesting discussions about life.

This picture shows a typical finca with a local country woman

One day, we all set off early and walked round the whole island, keeping as near to the coast as we could. Every so often as we looked down on the beach, we noticed a partly built hotel that David had co-designed with the team he was a part of.

One of the strangest experiences we had took place in the middle of the night. I was awoken suddenly by the light going on in our bedroom. I looked up and there was a man looking at me! In such extraordinary moments, I wrestle with complete disbelief and paralysis, unable to form a plan of action. In fear, I awoke David who also seemed momentarily stunned but then he leapt out of bed and the man ran away, through the next flat and over the balcony, seven floors up! We found out later that he made a point of visiting every woman who came to live on the island, and that one woman had actually woken in the night to find him in bed with her! I was so relieved not to have been living on my own.

I was enjoying teaching the locals and a German couple English. I didn't speak Spanish but I succeeded by learning the Spanish one chapter of the book ahead of the English I was teaching them. David was designing hotels and houses on the island's beach fronts and together we were saving up our earnings and hiding the cash under the sofa. After nearly six months of living like this, we began to get itchy feet and felt we needed to see more of the world. We decided to go on 'the hippie trail' and travel as far as possible overland to Kathmandu in Nepal.

David travelled back to England for an interview in Oxford for an architectural course and he obtained the necessary visas and inoculations for himself. On his way back, he happened to pass a Turkish shipping agency in the Ramblas in Barcelona. On impulse, he went in and booked tickets for a boat trip to Beirut in the Lebanon. When he told me what he'd done I was taken aback as we had not made a decision about when to travel and we would be leaving in a couple of weeks.

We made very few preparations: I was given a smallpox inoculation which I was to discover was totally ineffective but only after travelling through several countries where smallpox was endemic. We also sent off the addresses of all the Postes Restantes of the towns we intended to visit, including the British High

Commission in New Delhi, to our families in the hopes that they would write to us. We intended to return to England at the end of July in time for David's course.

Once we reached Lebanon, such a trip would entail travelling by ourselves, making our own decisions about the route to take, how to travel and where to stay from day to day with a view to arriving eventually in Kathmandu. John was also interested in making such a trip but he decided to go on ahead and meet us in India.

After pouring over the map showing the vast stretches of land and sea between where we were and where we were going, we made our decisions about which countries to go through. We didn't know at the time that some of our decisions would come to nothing because of political restrictions due to a country's unfriendly relations with England. We did know however that due to the war between Israel and Syria, we would not be able to visit Israel as that evidence in our passports would prevent us from then going through Syria and other Muslim countries.

The Journey

S o on **Wednesday 4th March 1970** we left our comfortable life in Ibiza for Barcelona where we were due to board the Turkish boat. I don't recall feeling anxious about what we were planning to do and perhaps the fact that we were blissfully unaware of the potential dangers was partly the reason for this. However, I noted in my journal that even only a few minutes away from Ibiza on the boat, the whole Ibizan experience seemed a long way away and became increasingly unreal the further away we sailed. I felt a few degrees under the weather, which I now know is what was happening when I had conflicting emotions that I was unaware of. Facing the unknown also made me hyper aware of everything.

I found Barcelona fascinating and probably much of it was very different from the way it is today. I loved the high buildings in the Spanish style with their balconies and green plants, the narrow, dark streets with shafts of sunlight glimmering here and there to light up a plant or a facade; ornate metal work and gorgeous tiles; the dark courtyards, sometimes palatial yet leading to inner squalid and dirty streets. I had never seen markets such as I saw there with so much quality produce of everything and so beautifully arranged.

The streets of Barcelona's red light area beckoned mysteriously, revealing neon signs and hundreds of bars emitting a red glow. At night, hoards of men flocked into the bars to take their positions at the bar with their drinks and turn to face the line of prostitutes opposite them and then apparently simply to leer at them. It was a strange scene. Certainly, the women were not beautiful but neither were the men. I wondered what was going on in each of their minds with so many possible hopes, fears, fantasies, longings and disappointments. Were the men actually going to hire a prostitute?

How did the women feel? Had all the myriad feelings and attitudes faded from the prostitutes' minds leaving nothing but boredom and the need to earn money?

Barcelona back street with atmospheric lighting

We spent much of our time going from bank to bank changing all our hard earned Spanish pesetas into U.S. dollars because we were only allowed to change a small amount at each one.

On the third day 6th March we boarded the Turkish boat, the Karadeniz which was to take a week to get to the Lebanon from where we would start our overland journey. Our trip was beginning.

It soon became obvious that we were a multicultural group of passengers living together in a relatively small space, something we had never experienced. All were men apart from me and one other woman. To sleep, everyone was crammed together in small dormitories with eight bunks, but for some reason, I was given a dormitory to myself: it seemed that the fact that David and I were married carried no weight here. Mainly, I enjoyed this as it gave me some quiet time to myself and privacy.

The only others who had English as their first language were two young, open-minded American men. There was a Lebanese male prostitute, several Egyptians, Turks, Iranians, Syrians, Palestinian and Jordanian refugees, Indians, a French man and a Mexican woman with an Armenian man. I had no idea where she was sleeping.

We immediately made friends with two Egyptian professionals who spoke English well. We particularly liked one of them. He was such a sensitive, deep thinking man and he opened our naive, parochial minds somewhat to the war in the Middle East from an educated, Egyptian viewpoint. He told us that the general population there did not want war at all and that many of them realised they were caught up in a conflict of power between other nations.

I don't remember him referring to internal power conflicts, but there was probably only a certain freedom he could allow himself in our discussions. He himself had suffered a personal and humiliating experience from the fallout of this war: he had been imprisoned in Israel and then ultimately left naked outside the prison without money to walk back barefoot to Egypt. Given such a traumatic occurrence, he was amazingly calm about the event, not using it as an excuse to sound off about the Israelis. He had a beautiful dignity. Because I was so ignorant of all that was going on in the Middle East, I wanted to hear an account from an Israeli too.

On 7th March we stopped over in Marseille. We were now in winter again which was rather a shock after the warm spring we'd been enjoying in Ibiza and we were frozen. Raw ice lay around the hyacinths and pansies and I'd had no opportunity to buy winter clothes. We didn't find it interesting in the short time we had to explore it but at least I found I had come out of my hyper-aware state and was more grounded.

On 8th March we called in at Genoa in a storm of hailstones where snow lay thick on the mountains. It looked a fascinating port, crowded with buildings rising up through the mists in front of the mountains, but even though the hail turned to rain and we ventured out, we felt too cold to do much exploring.

We were finding the other passengers friendly and interesting and we had many lively discussions. Sami invited us to join him for a time on Arwad - an island off Syria, - though we felt we wouldn't have time to accept this kind offer. Another Syrian from Damascus, Nazim, tried to educate us about the Arab people and the Muslim religion. He stressed how practical a religion it was and how forward thinking the Arab race was. He told us that the Turkish influence had not been good for them. He said it was their influence rather than that of the Arabs that kept women covering their faces. He told us that Christianity was wide-spread in Syria and Egypt and that even the Muslims were usually only taking one wife nowadays because the Koran stated that women must be given their rights. In more practical terms, and with just a hint of irony, he added that most men couldn't afford more than one wife anyway!

We knew practically nothing about the main religions of the world actually and which parts of the globe they were practised in, and it was on board this boat that we began our limited education. I found it fascinating. In those days, Christianity was the only religion taught in English schools and Jewish children were allowed to opt out of any teaching or assemblies.

We learnt from Nazim that religion and culture were closely linked. Islam was practised by Muslims in Syria, especially in Damascus he said, and in Turkey, Egypt, Jordan, Saudi Arabia, Sudan, Iran, Afghanistan, Pakistan and Iraq to mention just some of the countries. Their prophet was known as Mohammed. Buddhism was practised in countries such as Tibet, Thailand, Burma and Ceylon, as Sri Lanka was called in those days. A mixture of Buddhism and Hinduism was practised in Nepal. Hinduism was the main religion of India where the one God known as Brahman is the cause and foundation of all existence. Three principal gods that are expressions of Brahman help him in this: Brahma, who creates the universe, Vishnu, who preserves the universe and Shiva, who destroys the universe.

On Monday 9th March the sun came out at last and we arrived at the huge port of Naples. The previous night the weather had been stormy which had delayed us in having the time we needed to go into the museum where many of the volcanic relics from Pompeii were to be seen.

Discussions about Egyptian society continued with our doctor friend. As he was so educated and as we had no knowledge of any of this ourselves we took what he told us on trust. He said that the medical service was free and that education was free for all children and that for the very bright, education was compulsory to the age of twenty one. Then they would have another six years or so of training in their chosen profession, plus a year or eighteen months of military service. After all this, they were still liable to be called up for another six more years of service until they reached the age of forty. Consequently, the most educated men did not marry till the age of thirty.

Working class men, on the other hand, only had two compulsory years of military service and up to four more years at the most. It seemed that the terms 'educated' and 'bright' were considered synonymous. He thought that 80% of all young people were educated up to the age of about twenty. Girls were now encouraged to be in competition with the boys and were welcomed into most jobs. He said that the universities accepted Arabs from all countries, and the University for Muslims in Cairo was called El-Azhar.

He also added to our utter amazement that many Egyptian men would still kill their wives if they were unfaithful, and one of the Egyptian men we met told us that he would end the marriage if he so much as saw his wife talking to another man! Yet women were encouraged to cut down on the size of their families with contraceptive pills, and to have only one or two children.

It was also very interesting to have their Arab take on the Israel - Arab war. He acknowledged that it was a dangerous situation and that it seemed insoluble. Personally, I had first been aware of its existence in 1956 when I set off for a Guide camp. As my father saw me off, he had told me that he might be called up to fight in this war to protect the Suez Canal and keep it open for shipping. He had left me in some anxiety, wondering if I would ever see him again. I am glad to say that although I believe England was on the brink of war, it did not happen. More recently, David and I had become aware that the conflict had escalated into war again and it was not far from our minds on our journey up to and through the Middle East.

Our Egyptian friend gave us a simplified history of the conflict and the complications of the Palestinian situation and the cold war between Russia and the West, particularly America. He didn't mention Britain in his account, perhaps out of tact. He said that America was supplying arms to Israel and putting in a lot of money to train their armed forces. Russia was supplying arms and training to Egypt but was less wealthy. He told us that it had started when Jews came from all over the world and settled in Palestine to have their own place. They bought up land bit by bit, turned the poor Palestinians away from their country and called the land Israel. However, they were and still are surrounded by enemies. They continued to try and claim more and more Arab land for territorial advantage which was, he said, how the war had started.

He acknowledged that the Arabs were split in how they felt the problem should be resolved. Some felt that Jews should not be allowed to stay in Israel as they could simply never be trusted. Others felt it would be possible for the Jews to stay there if the Palestinians were allowed to return to form a new country together and call it by a different name. Trust in such a geo-politically hot situation was clearly well-nigh impossible to re-establish.

Our Egyptian friend added that the Six Day War of 1967, also known as the third Arab-Israeli War, was really a trick from a double agent where the Egyptian leaders were told to go back and leave Sinai, so were not prepared for the fighting that ensued, and the Israeli forces came in and took over the area. They had taken control of the Gaza Strip and the Sinai Peninsula from Egypt, the West Bank and east Jerusalem from Jordan, and the Golan Heights from Syria. He added that all the Egyptian leaders had subsequently mysteriously disappeared and it was widely believed that they had been assassinated.

The evening hit a lighter note after our evening meal with the intervention of a young Arab man. He had let it be known to the other Arabs on board that he lived in Quebec and had pretended that he was not Arab himself and could not speak Arabic. He designed beautiful jewellery and seemed also to enjoy weaving imaginative fantasies.

He told everyone that he lived in a nudist colony where everyone swapped wives, bringing some of the other Arabs into the conversation to shock them. He would speak in English to us, translate it into French to the French man, all the time understanding what the Arabs were discussing among themselves and intentionally misunderstanding their response! It was actually excruciatingly funny, but we felt we had to hide our hilarity because the Arabs had been so very kind to us. One of the Egyptians got so worked up that we feared some trouble would erupt before we landed again on the Thursday.

In fact, tensions soon evaporated and on Tuesday 10th March I commented to David that there was a quite a sense of unity amongst this multi-national group of passengers. We reflected on the difference between this and how things were between the Great Powers and the outcomes of their political machinations. The Arabs were remarkably warm and hospitable with us and many of them invited us to stay at their homes. We should love to have accepted the invitations from the Egyptians but David didn't think we had the time to stay there. We did however arrange to visit the separate homes of two Syrians and we were given the name of someone else to visit in Aleppo.

Our discussions of Muslim life continued. As far as I know, suicide bombing was unheard of in those times. We learnt that they prayed five times a day for a few minutes, using whatever passage from the Koran they liked. Their essential message was that they should be good and that goodness breeds goodness. They commented that younger people were not as devout as the older generations and didn't have the time to pray so often. They also said that the government was apt to twist the meaning of the Koran for its own benefit.

All this immersion in Eastern life was interrupted in the evening by the showing of an American film which we very much enjoyed watching: 'The Good, The Bad and the Ugly' starring Clint Eastwood. Films from the west were to play some part in our sense of the strangeness of two cultures coming together as we travelled further east.

The food that we were given on board this ship was out of this world as far as we were concerned. Turkish food was not found in England as it is today, and we were told that it was one of the five main cuisines of the world. None of the crew spoke English but we tried to convey to them how much we appreciated it. The only problem was that we were expected to eat all five courses in about fifteen minutes! We were treated to two main meals like this each day. It was a sacrilege to have to gulp down such delicious food so quickly.

As the following day Wednesday 11ᵗʰ March was the last day the Egyptians would be on board, we played games in the evening. We started off with card games, then the sort of party games that we hadn't played since we were children! It was great fun and they always seemed to know exactly when to change the game before we'd had too much of it.

At times, I felt nervous about being in a dormitory on my own with David in quite another part of the boat with the other male passengers. One of the crew members had his room more or less opposite mine. Perhaps he was there to make sure that I was safe but I felt disturbed by the near naked pinups on full view on his walls. It made it difficult to relax. That night the weather was extremely rough and it was impossible to sleep anyway. My rucksack rolled from one side of the cabin dormitory to the other, crashing into the different beds with every wave. The following morning, I was too sea-sick to get up and I was given my breakfast in bed.

On Thursday 12th March we arrived at Alexandria and were very sad to say goodbye to the Egyptians and hoped we would meet up again one day.

Typical backstreet scene in Alexandria with a picture of Gamal Abdul Nasser who was the current president.

We had a little time to explore the port and felt excited to know that it was the first time that we had set foot on African soil. It had such a foreign feel for us. We saw so much poverty and misery there that after our talks with our privileged Egyptian friends we realised the extremes must be great in Egypt. Apparently, people did not have the freedom to choose how much they charged for their goods as the government decided this. We had been told that it would be a good idea for us to buy a watch there, but ironically, we did not have the time!

We started off our visit by having lunch with three of our Arab friends from the ship: Sami, Nazim and Khalid. We had a typical Egyptian meal of brown beans in garlic sauce with a side dish of salad and bean fritters mashed and shaped into balls and fried: lovely but filling. Our Egyptian friends had not told us that we should never eat salad in Egypt. Perhaps it never occurred to them that anyone would do such a thing but the Arab friends with us didn't mention it either. As it was, David and I had felt very queasy and had an upset stomach for days afterwards. We put this down to the food being too rich for our stomachs. However, it is possible that this meal was also responsible for some later health issues but then so could much other food or drink that we were to consume on our travels. After the meal, we set off to explore Alexandria on our own.

There were ten miles of beach but the tide was right up to the wall. We couldn't believe that anyone could survive the driving which was crazy and appeared chaotic. So many people, who presumably could not afford to pay for the fare to travel inside the buses, were hanging from them that they looked as though they could bring the bus down on top of them. There were many beggars too. You could buy thirst quenching drinks made from freshly squeezed oranges at road side stalls or drinks made from carrots or from sugar cane.

We came across a military building at one point and David was starting to put his camera to his eye when a soldier raised his rifle at him! It was a very new world to us which hinted at possible dangers to come.

We got back to the boat to discover that there were two new passengers: English women. It was rare to find English travellers so far afield in those days and these women were quite amazing. They were nurses and had been working in the United Nations hospital in Jordan for refugees under terrible conditions. Their only help had been from untrained women who it seemed had no patience. The doctors only ever discussed the conditions of the patients without ever prescribing anything. Presumably, there was no money to buy medicine or other necessities.

Eventually, the women had decided to move on and had journeyed to India and back by bus and train. We were in great admiration of them and so interested to hear something about the sort of journey that we were embarking on. They gave us several tips and influenced our journey yet again. We were constantly changing our minds about our route according to what other travellers were telling us.

We had several more invitations to visit the Arabs on the boat and although we should have loved to do so, it was unlikely that we could fit them all in. We were overwhelmed by their warm hearts.

On Friday 13th March our Turkish boat trip came to an end at Beirut in the Lebanon, the beginning of our overland journey. Setting off, however, was not a simple matter. We spent half a day, waiting for immigration officials, customs officials, police and the army to check our documents and allow us into the Lebanon. We found the customs officials made quite a song and dance about searching everyone but of course we hadn't got used to the fact that we were in a dangerous part of the world.

We were shocked by the apparent craziness of the city. It was loud, hip and cosmopolitan, with many of the Arabs speaking American English. The driving, much of which was in American cars, was even more frightening than in Alexandria with their horns sounding non-stop to forestall danger rather than adhering to any safe traffic rules! Nazim told us that it was far more expensive to stay here than in Syria so we decided to push on.

We took an Impala taxi to Damascus over snow-clad mountains with Khalid – a Jordanian / Palestinian refugee and Nazim who was also a Palestinian refugee and who lived in Damascus.

It was comforting to be travelling with Arabs who knew the score. We arrived there late into the night. Luckily, we didn't have any trouble obtaining a visa on the Lebanon / Syria border and this time it was a quick matter to get through customs. We had a delicious Syrian sandwich which was like a large pancake spread with yogurt and rolled up. We found a youth hostel called the Barada Hostel for the equivalent price of about two old shillings each a night and went straight to bed.

The following morning 14th March Khalid and Nazim came to the hotel and we started our tour of Damascus. Because of the Middle Eastern troubles, tourists were a rarity and we found ourselves the objects of curiosity: with my blonde hair, I was sometimes at the other end of a camera. In old Damascus, we walked down the Roman street called Straight which is mentioned in the book of Acts in the Bible when recording the conversion of St Paul. We wandered through a famous and ancient market and our senses were thrilled by the bombardment of new and exotic sights and smells.

I should have loved to buy some of the gorgeous hand-woven silks but we had to be very careful with our money in order to be able to continue our travels. We were also surprised by the number of westernised goods on show. Many of the Arab women were covered in black veils and it was amusing to our western eyes to watch a woman eating an ice cream under her veil.

We then went on to the beautiful Umayyad Mosque in the old city also known as the Great Mosque of Damascus, described as 'the greatest erection built in the Islam territory'. It is one of the largest and oldest mosques in the world and is perhaps considered the fourth holiest place in Islam. The Umayyad Mosque apparently stands on the site of a 1st-century Hellenic temple to Jupiter and of a later Christian Basilica dedicated to John the Baptist, who is honoured by both Christians and Muslims. His head was found in a box during the mosque's construction and it is believed that it now lies in a shrine inside the mosque. The mosque was an innovation in Islamic building, using mosaics lavishly on the outside and was built in 705 AD by 12,000 skilled specialists who came from all over the Arab world.

Typical mosaic decoration of the Umayyad Mosque.

We admired the mosaics so much that our friends took us to the factory where craftsmen made the mosaics to replace damaged ones or ones that had come away from the walls. They gave us two pieces of coloured glass used for the mosaics and also made us a cup of tea. They told us that one of the mosaic designs had apparently won first prize in a competition in Barcelona.

We then went on to the Azem Palace close by the mosque which was built by the Turks in 1749 originally as a residence for the Ottoman governor of Damascus. Although it was now a museum I believe, it was set up as though still used for its original purpose. I loved the peaceful atmosphere of the courtyards with their elegant ponds and fountains.

https://en.wikipedia.org/wiki/**Azm_Palace**

"The architecture is an excellent example of Damascene traditional houses. The structure itself consists of several buildings and two wings: the harem and the selamlik. The harem is the family wing, which is a private space for the residents (originally, the Azem family). This wing included the kitchen, servant quarters, and the baths, which are a replica of the public baths in the city but on a smaller scale. The selamlik is the guest wing, and it comprises the formal halls, reception areas and large courtyards with traditional cascading fountains.

Used in the building of this palace were several types of stones including limestone, sandstone, basalt, and marble, chosen to provide a natural decoration for the structure."

Inside, the rooms were spacious and the ceilings had wooden panels that were painted with natural scenes. Although I found it incredibly lavish and beautiful, it did not seem too opulent. I loved the inlaid ivory and mother of pearl that was used to decorate the furniture; the beautiful vases, lamps and brass light fittings. The reddish brown, blue, green and gold colours went so well together.

Unfortunately, Khalid had to get back to Jordan after showing us these wonderful delights of ancient Syria, and we weren't sure if we'd ever see him again. Nazim invited us to visit his family the next day which we were really looking forward to.

At 10:30 a.m. on Sunday 15th March Nazim came to collect us to take us to his home. We met his brother and also his young sister who was in army training uniform, such training now being a compulsory part of the school curriculum. His mother was also present as were two friends who spoke English really well. One of them had studied in England. The other was a strong supporter of El Fata. We spent over five hours with them and were treated to a beautiful meal there with many exotic dishes that we had never tasted before.

Our conversation covered many topics but it was mainly about their people and the war which understandably preoccupied their lives. Because my understanding of the historical situation was minimal I was shocked when they told us that Britain had given Israel to the Jews after the Second World War. This really hit my conscience and I wondered if governments considered all possible outcomes to the decisions they made. Perhaps it was strange that I should feel guilty about a historical decision that I had played no part in but travellers from Britain were so rare in that part of the world that I felt in some small way that we were ambassadors for England and therefore that we carried a responsibility.

The main thrust of our friends' comments was that they had very little going for them compared with the Israelis: they said that their people had been asleep for too long, that they did not manufacture their own weapons, except for a few in Egypt, they were not given the training that the Israelis received and that Russia was not helping them in the way that America helped the Israelis. They commented on the fact that Jews were both strong and well educated and that every man, woman and child there was trained to be a fighter. They felt that the Arabs were beginning to wake up and that the Syrians, Jordanians as well as Palestinian refugees were willing to sacrifice their lives to give back 'Palestine' to her people. Syria had begun to train their women and children to fight as they believed that Israel wanted to take possession of Damascus.

At 4:30 pm we left his home, mother and sister and walked around parts of the town. We saw the university which apparently took 40,000 students and we looked at new housing projects. In the evening, we sat in a cafe for hours and continued our immersion into the plight of the Arabs. We heard a new viewpoint from one of the men but had no idea how many other Arabs shared it. He said that the Jews wanted this land in Syria so that they could form a central network and be really powerful. He said that their aim was not just to conquer the Arabs but that one day they would even turn against America. He feared that the conflict could even result in another war between America and Russia.

He told us that Egyptian bookshops were filled with books on Communism. I reflected that Israel was certainly in an amazingly powerful geographical position situated between the East and the West: powerful yet for that very reason also vulnerable. I guessed that fear was as much a part of their psyche as for the Arabs and similarly could lead to paranoid thinking and action which was as much defensive as aggressive.

Our Arab hosts also reminded us that this was essentially a holy war, though Arabs had been long-time neighbours with Jews and that there were many Jewish Arabs. The situation was so complex. They said it was Zionism that the Arabs were really fighting: the Jews wanting to take over land where Jews from all over the world could come and settle.

We were still sitting in the cafe at 9:30 pm when we saw flares, and our Arab friends told us that they were fireworks. They probably said this to put our minds at rest, but a moment later, we were in a blackout. We heard planes flying over Damascus and our friends looked as worried as we were. They took hold of our hands because it was so dark and ran back to our hostel with us. As soon as we arrived, we learnt that Israeli planes had bombed a military base near the border with the Lebanon and that they had killed five soldiers and wounded seventeen. This was the closest they had ever come to Damascus and they were obviously planning something. It was frightening for the Arabs, and David and I felt afraid too.

The following day 16th March I was in a quandary. The Syrian planes had been flying over Damascus all morning and we were sure that there was danger ahead. We knew it would be wise to leave Damascus but David was ill: he had fainted and been unconscious for some time. Nazim had arranged to meet us at 10 a.m. but had not turned up. We realised that day that we had not taken the sort of precautions we should have to protect ourselves from getting ill. Not only had we been drinking the water since we boarded the Turkish boat but we had also been eating raw vegetables. We simply had had no idea of the risks that we were taking. I think this was partly because we had set off from Ibiza rather than from England where I imagine we would have been given some advice.

I stayed in our simple hostel near David all day, courted by the hotel manager, given two Syrian sandwiches at lunch time and taught Arabic numerals. By 9 p.m. still none of our Arab friends had turned up and we reasoned that either they too were ill or they had decided that it wasn't wise to be seen with us by other Arabs now that it looked as though the war could be restarting.

The next morning Tuesday 17th March I awoke with another upset stomach. David, on the other hand, was feeling a lot better and so we decided that we shouldn't risk another day in Damascus. We left our hotel, sad not to be able to say our goodbyes to our kind Arab friends, and caught a bus north to Hama. You can just make me out in the front seat of the bus.

Our bus stopped for petrol in Homs heading north towards Hama.

We set off but we wondered when we would ever start on the journey proper as the driver spent ages going round and round the city until the bus was full. He checked everyone who boarded the bus and threw off the child beggars. Once he had been paid and things seemed calmer we thought that we would be leaving at last but the call to prayer blared out loudly from the radio. I found this to be the most beautiful and spine-tingling sound that I had ever heard in my life. Many of the Muslims got out of the bus and unrolled their prayer mats and prostrated themselves, facing in the direction of Mecca.

Once everyone was back on the bus, the driver turned on the engine and we were on our way. The long bus trip bombarded my senses with new images, sounds and smells, but it was the noise that provided the greatest onslaught. It sounded as though the bus's engine had never been tuned or perhaps had been tuned to create the greatest noise possible. In competition with this sound, the driver turned up the volume on the radio to play what I assumed was the Koran being sung, but I wasn't sure. Every few seconds he used his foot to hoot his horn in the face of the chaos that was life on the road to Hama. With each hoot, the Arabs on the bus said a prayer to Allah. We wondered what our chances were of arriving at our destination in one piece!

The season was changing again and it grew warmer. Country Arabs in their flowing robes and headgear, wandered around at a leisurely pace by the road side and on the road, sometimes riding on a donkey. Some shepherds were trying to control flocks of sheep and goats. Sometimes they were praying. We passed one woman who had prostrated herself on top of a mound of earth: perhaps a grave. Further away, we admired trees with their pink and white blossom, maybe almond and fruit trees, and in the distance, the soft pale mountains with a sort of coxcomb ridge. It was wondrous, as though scenes from the Bible had come alive.

After the mountains, the further north we travelled, the richer the earth became, turning black ultimately. Along the Asi River Valley, the sun shone on lush green plains and neat cultivated fields watered by the rains from the Lebanese mountains. There were a few clumps of trees, - withies, silver birches and blossom trees. We were in spring once again. It was all very beautiful. As David put it so well, 'Perhaps this is Paradise, but still the Syrian Migs fly overhead!'

Occasionally, we passed stone villages with low, pale houses, very close together with small windows, as much a part of the earth as the rest of the landscape. We were in the land that Jesus had lived in and I had the feeling that life had changed very little.

Once we reached Hama, and were enjoying a wonderful warm temperature somewhere in the seventies Fahrenheit (21 to 26 degrees Celsius), we took a taxi to the home of another Arab we'd met on the boat which turned out to be a mansion. Considering that his father had a prominent position in Hama, it was not surprising. He drove us around the city for a while and pointed out the amazing water wheels, said to have been built in Roman times, though the ones we saw which were still working had been built in the middle ages. They irrigated the land by taking water up and along irrigation channels leading to the fields. There were seventeen of them and they were huge: approximately fifty feet in diameter. As they turned, they made a strange moaning sound, very eerie. especially at night time. He told us, 'If you were a true citizen of Hama, you were born within the creaking sound of the water wheels.'

The water wheels of Hama

When we returned to his home, we were treated to a lot of rich food including a dessert made of sweet cheese and nuts. Normally we would have appreciated this so much but our stomachs were still suffering. It was impossible even to begin to do justice to this wonderful spread feeling so queasy. It seemed rude and ungrateful to our hosts when they had gone to so much trouble and it seemed difficult for them to understand or accept our explanation.

We found it challenging to communicate with them generally, **and the following morning, 18ᵗʰ March,** after seeing another opulent and lovely Azem Palace built for the same Ottoman governor As'ad Pasha al-Azem as the palace in Damascus, we decided to press on to Aleppo, the northern capital of Syria. En route, we passed villages with homes that seemed to be part of the land with their organic shapes that looked like mud bee hives.

When we got to Aleppo it began to rain and we noticed that it was much colder again here. We decided to take up the invitation to visit Daniel, the Armenian refugee friend we'd made on the boat, though we had no idea what to expect. He and his family proved to be the kindest we'd ever met and we were treated as guests of honour. We soon learnt that we could not express our admiration for anything they owned or they would tell us to take it! They cooked wonderful meals and even gave up their double bed for us, where we slept soundly, watched over by a large illuminated cross.

Daniel showed us around Aleppo which was bigger than Damascus and in fact the largest city in Syria. However, there was a much smaller Arab population here with something of a European influence present. We couldn't place the architecture and it was full of shops, quite a few cinemas and parks. We discovered the reason for this difference was that thousands of Armenians lived there and half the total population were Catholics. Few of the women were veiled. I rather missed the flowing robes of the Arab men and the beautiful ornate dresses of the women of Hama.

Even here, we realised that there were hardly ever any tourists. Every time we ever stopped in Syria for whatever reason, we were surrounded by groups of curious locals, and in Aleppo, they were asking Daniel about us. In the evening we were treated to many cakes and drinks and called into a cafe where a rather strange and bashful young man treated us to drinks, nuts and biscuits and declared his love for David!

The following day Thursday 19th March it rained and David especially was getting itchy feet for the journey ahead. We had planned to travel to Iraq next, taking the night train to Baghdad, but on going to the Iraqi Embassy, we discovered that the Americans, Germans and British needed a fortnight to obtain a visa. We decided therefore to go north into Turkey and on to Iran instead.

Daniel helped us to arrange for a taxi to take us to the Syrian / Turkish border. Meanwhile, we were tempted to buy some of the beautiful things that we saw. I should have loved a very old coffee pot which cost 20 Syrian pounds (just under £2 in old English money), but it would have been impossible to carry and in the end, we were seduced by the old silver jewellery in the ancient covered market. For 50 Syrian pounds, I bought two necklaces, one of which was antique. They decided on the price by weighing them rather than by their antique value.

I also bought a loose, brown cotton top with yellow embroidery for when the warmer weather arrived. I had no clothes for the frequent change of seasons that we were going to encounter on this trip. I was treated to a wash and set by Daniel's cousin who was a hairdresser. This was fun and unexpected. Later, we went on to his cousin's family who kindly treated us to a typical Syrian meal of shish kebabs cooked over charcoal with something that looked like tapioca balls filled with brown beans, flat bread, some vegetables and yogurt with a pale sauce made from aubergines.

On Friday 20ᵗʰ March we decided to see the Citadel of Aleppo, a large medieval fortified palace in the centre of the old city.

https://en.wikipedia.org/wiki/Citadel_of_Aleppo

'It is considered to be one of the oldest and largest castles in the world. Usage of the Citadel hill dates back at least to the middle of the 3rd millennium BC. Subsequently occupied by many civilizations including the Greeks, Byzantines, Ayyubids and Mamluks, the majority of the construction as it stands today is thought to originate from the Ayyubid period.' .... This was when *'Saladin's son al-Zahir al-Ghazi ruled Aleppo between 1193 and 1215.'*

The throne room was in wonderful condition with a beautiful ceiling and stained glass windows, and the provision for the defenders was remarkable in that it was built so that they were safe from attack from all conceivable angles.

Citadel of Aleppo

Daniel showed us the doorway to the Hittite temple, which he said was originally built to the sun god around 2000 BC. There must have been a lot of restoration work done.

We returned for lunch, then made our farewells to this kind family when our taxi arrived at 2:30 p.m. to take us to Turkey. Daniel insisted on paying the fare in advance. I felt overwhelmed by his generosity and we knew it would help us to make the most of our money in terms of how far we could travel.

Syria had been a very interesting experience. There were beautiful sites and architecture there that had been seen by relatively few people from the outside world, the legacy of wonderful crafts and ancient knowledge passed from generation to generation. There was much kindness too from the Arabs, whether they were Christian or Muslim. We were not sure how much formal education there was for many of its people, and apart from Aleppo, there was little sign of wealth or progress as the economy had been taken up with the conflict with Israel. How tragic this was! This war continued to occupy my mind on and off during and after my journey and came to the forefront when I later met an Israeli in India.

Many Arabs just seemed to wander around in an aimless fashion, though of course they might also have had purpose but without the time constraints of the western world. I reflected that it is all too easy for us in the west to judge other ways as inferior when there might well be advantages as well as disadvantages to living in a different way. Why are changes and our own ways always considered to be a form of progress? The hippy movement had sprung from the dissatisfaction with the capitalism of the western world where making money seemed to be the prime motivator rather than the values of care and compassion. Of course, this movement had also gone hand in hand with naivety and the lack of knowledge of how to sustain and make practical such a visionary ideology.

However, we did not cross the border at Kirikhan which we had planned to do and David had his first real experience of trying to bargain with the driver, but without success. Without the language, it was impossible to know the reason for the driver's decision not to take us where we wanted to go. Anyway, we were lucky in finding a taxi on the Turkish side that took us on to Kirikhan and to a minibus that was actually on the point of leaving for Gaziantep.

The journey was scheduled to take three hours but the state of the bus made this impossible. It was a rickety piece of machinery and it broke down several times in the mountains, occasionally enveloping us in smoke from the exhaust. However, after our time in Syria it was so interesting to notice the difference in the nature of the people and the countryside, in this part of Turkey anyway. They were not openly hostile to us but even though they stared at us they did not try to communicate or even smile. There were mainly men travelling. They wore flat caps and their faces remained blank and empty in spite of the potential danger, and they all smoked strong-smelling tobacco non-stop.

The countryside was naturally green from all the rain and we were in a more mountainous part of Turkey with rivers, streams and trees. There were occasional buildings, sometimes with thatched and sometimes pitched roofs. The people in the villages also wore flat caps and there were horse-drawn carts. In the middle of nowhere, we ran out of petrol and waited for an hour with ten Turks who were as miserable as we were in the cold!

We arrived at Gaziantep, a small market town, and were led to the square and taken to a simple hotel where we were shown a room. About twelve men followed us in and formed a silent circle around us. They were clearly interested in me and I suppose they had never seen a young blonde woman before. We were unsure of their motivation or what we should do in this situation but suddenly, an idea came to me. I stepped forward and one by one, I shook the hand of each of the men in a purposeful way, dismissing each as I turned to the next. Luckily, the message seemed to get through and we were relieved to see them gradually disperse and leave the room.

The following day 21ˢᵗ March at 11:30 a.m. we began our eighteen hour journey by bus to Erzurum. We were now deep into a freezing winter. After Elazig, we climbed into the snow-covered mountains and the journey was slow and hazardous. We were soon driving along narrow mountain roads, zigzagging around steep passes with deep ravines just wide enough for single vehicles. At one point, we travelled through a pass, high up in the clouds, watching white walls of snow on either side of us twice the height of the bus.

It snowed heavily through the night, sometimes pelting the roof of the bus with hail, and the driver had to negotiate deep drifts which he did with great skill. Luckily a snow plough was at work to cope with the worst of them and we realised that we were very lucky to be able to get through at all. We learnt later that all the passengers and the driver of the bus that had made this journey the previous week had frozen to death when the bus broke down! Luckily we had not known this when we set off.

Perhaps the Turkish people who were travelling with us already knew the danger. They certainly seemed indifferent, cold even towards each other as well as us. It was difficult to know if it was a cultural trait and just in this part of Turkey or to do with the current weather. The music that blared out unceasingly from the radio had self-pitying refrains. As I looked around at the barrenness of the mud villages, and the cold without comfort, I could certainly understand how they could be affected in this way.

In the villages there were children everywhere, often very young, out in the cold selling things. They looked like miniature adults rather in the way that the Victorian children of England had. Every time the bus stopped and we got out to stretch our legs, people formed a group in front of us simply staring with blank expressions. At one point, we entered a sort of cafe where there were rugs rolled up at the edges of the room and we all sat on the floor leaning against them. Another time, a sailor, who spoke three words of English, gave us some tea, which was really welcome. Another passed around some biscuits, but this did not invoke any form of gratitude or communication from the other passengers. It was all rather surreal.

We arrived at the dingy town of Erzurum at 5:30 a.m. on 22nd March in the cold and snow and managed to catch a bus half an hour later to the equally desolate and dirty town of Agri. Men with their animals wandered around looking miserable and worn down and we noticed that some of the carts had solid, wooden wheels rather than tyres.

We caught a minibus at 6 a.m. and travelled through this desolate, flat wasteland while the snow blew horizontally around us. We passed several more impoverished villages with mud houses and smoke coming from holes in the roofs till we arrived at the Turkish / Iranian border. It was now 2:30 p.m. This was the bleakest of wastelands we had yet seen. It occurred to me that this must be Hades with its winter of eternal darkness. Somehow, we had unknowingly left the world of the living and entered the world of the dead.

I recalled that God brought the flood to this part of the world because he was displeased with the people, according to the account in the book of Genesis. En route we had passed close to the southern slopes of Mount Ararat where it was said that Noah's ark came to rest after God had warned Noah what he needed to do to save himself and each kind of animal. The mountain was covered in snow.

There we were lucky to meet a French couple who knew of a late bus to the nearby village of Maku over the border in Iran. Consequently, we were saved from having to spend the night in a disgusting and high-priced hotel on the Turkish side. Again, there was a noticeable change in the character of the people. The Iranians were lively, seemed brighter and had a lot of fun at the expense of the feelings of a village simpleton who was travelling on the bus with us.

Once we had found the hotel, several men surrounded us and the French couple to see what we would sell of our belongings. They wanted anything at all and were very business-like. Really, we had been carrying as little as possible and needed everything we had but eventually we got a room free for the night by David selling his shoes!

By then we were feeling uncomfortably dirty, not having had a private place to wash in since we were at Gaziantep. There was no private bathroom in this hotel either. My memory is that there was not even a door for the toilet and David had to stand on guard whenever I needed to use it. Perhaps no woman had ever entered the hotel and possibly Iranian women would not have even been allowed to. There was no lock on our bedroom door, so David did what he could with a piece of string and we slept with our money under the pillows beneath our heads. We had been travelling slowly for thirty hours continuously with little food and only the occasional doze. However, this was not a relaxing situation to say the least and sleep was difficult to come by.

David had a lot of pleasure from often pouring over our world map and wanted to travel as far and as fast as we could. Every night since we had boarded the Turkish boat, he would look at the distance we had travelled that day and feel a sense of achievement. He would also see how far we still had to travel to get to

Kathmandu. This was the place in Nepal that was somehow imbued with magnetism for young travellers and to which we also were drawn. From the kind of upbringing I had been given and being steeped in non-church Christian Science I recall that for the most part I had an accepting sense of whatever he decided.

It was now Monday 23rd March and we were aiming for Teheran. At 7:30 a.m. we caught the bus from Maku to Tabriz, going south again, and were soon on open plains, with rolling countryside and high, narrow mud walls dividing the fields. There were snowy mountains on either side of us, and camels grazing quietly or plodding along in trains. Our hearts lifted. We were not going to languish in Hades for ever more. Spring had come yet again as we approached Tabriz and it was a joy to see the blossom on the trees and to feel some warmth.

We were so relieved that the music on this bus neither had the same miserable refrains as the Turkish music nor was it played so loudly. The Iranian people here also laughed a lot with each other and did not stare at us so much. We also detected a rather ruthless streak in them.

Again, we were lucky in catching another bus at Tabriz at 12:30 pm, only half an hour after arriving there. In fact, we took the last two spare seats, and it might well have been that the buses only ever set off for their destination when they were full. In that case, we were relieved not to be sitting on a motionless bus for the day waiting for other passengers. We were always conscious that our money could only stretch so far so we avoided as many hotel stopovers as we could but the travelling was relentless. I was looking forward to a rest in Teheran.

The road to Teheran followed a river and was in a better state than previous roads except for the last part of the journey. However, my bottom was getting very sore from constant uncomfortable sitting. I couldn't wait for the opportunity to stretch my legs in Teheran. People on the back row beside us eventually offered us sweets which we gladly accepted. The scenery was unexciting to me: mountainous and mostly arid, relieved occasionally by camel trains, single camels and sheep and goats grazing.

We reached Teheran at 10:30 that night. We had travelled hundreds of miles over a period of three and a half days and we were feeling quite weak. We found a simple place to stay called the Baghdad Hostel, and we really liked the way the single rooms were built around the oriental courtyard and enjoyed the smell of incense that pervaded the place. Even the huge beetle I took out of my bed could not spoil this experience for me.

We started off the next day 24th March well with a fantastic shower. How important such things become when you can't get them easily and how grateful we felt! We were also happy to have left winter and be back in spring yet again. However, I became increasingly upset walking around Teheran with all the men hissing at me, touching and hitting me. One swiped angrily at my head with a newspaper.

At the time, I didn't realise that my head should be covered, but from this experience I guessed that the appearance of a western woman and particularly one with my sort of hair so openly walking on their streets was considered an outrage to their thinking. Yet the place was full of contradictions, ambivalence and conflict about western ways. Many Islamic women were wearing the veil but we were astonished to see some of the younger women wearing a transparent veil that not only did not cover the face but also revealed that they were wearing makeup, high heels and mini-skirts! It was far more alluring than if they had no veil at all.

The British Embassy was a modern, rather palatial building and though the officials seemed efficient they sent us in the wrong direction for the Afghanistan Embassy to obtain a visa for entry there and consequently we searched for a long time. However, this proved to be a blessing in disguise as while we were on this quest, we saw two modern, unveiled girls and asked them if they knew the way there. They didn't but they took us home with them to ask their parents who told us that all embassies were closed for the Nowruz Festival (their New Year feast) and we ended up being invited to stay with them.

There were three daughters there, one son, a son-in-law and the mother's mother. They were clearly well off with a lovely house, and after giving us lunch, they drove us to our hotel to collect our luggage. They were very kind to us and it was such a good experience to live in an Iranian home and talk with educated people about their country. It also felt strange in this place of comfort and modernity to know that we were surrounded by hundreds of miles of desolate land.

They told us that the teenagers were watching European and American films on television that showed all our western ways and freedoms. Night clubs had sprung up and the young were going dancing there. They thought about fifty percent of teenagers were modern, but our own impressions were that far more were traditional, at least from the point of view of wearing a veil. Education was very expensive so only the rich were educated and therefore able to think more independently. There was a university here, but no jobs for the graduates. Although many would have liked to leave the country, the government made it hard for them to do so by charging a lot of money for passports and even more for visas.

Our young friends took us to a very neat, formal park, and in the evening we went to the nearby American Marine Base. The marines were very hospitable to us as well and said we could go round there any time and have meals with them. We talked to one of the marines who had fought in Vietnam. He said he'd been there for eighteen months and that it was the best time of his life, but only in retrospect! He often hadn't enjoyed it at the time but on looking back, he realised how much it had matured him. Being in close proximity to men in the difficult conditions they shared had made him understand human nature better. Also, because he had felt death so close to him, it had helped him to appreciate life more deeply.

He became very upset when I told him about the two American guys we had met who said they would refuse call-up. To him, they were refusing to give back to their country even though they had received free education, while the people the marines were fighting for in Vietnam would have loved the education and were losing their lives. His reasoning as to why the USA was involved in this war didn't sound very convincing to me however. He said that the Vietnamese people needed the USA because they had no education and would make the wrong choice if left to themselves. I guessed it was one point of view but it seemed to lack the complexity that really lay behind America's choice to get involved in this war. He added that the American soldiers had great respect for the South Vietnamese soldiers because they fought cleanly, unlike the Viet Cong.

The following day 25th March one of the sisters took us down town to the museum and we were particularly impressed with the pottery there. We also visited the covered market but I felt rather uneasy in the midst of so many people, knowing how the men behaved with a western woman. Our friend bought me a pretty silk scarf.

In the afternoon, we had the strange experience of going up town to a discotheque which had a 'tea and dancing' session. It was dark and modern and full of fashionable young people. It seemed so charmingly innocent somehow to drink tea, eat cake and dance to heavy rock music. It was wonderful to hear one of my favourite bands, Led Zeppelin, in this surprising and divided city.

Continuing the strangely disorientating western experiences, we stayed in during the evening and watched 'Peyton Place' on television. I wondered if they thought that the films they saw on television were a true reflection of western life, but then we too were making generalisations about life and the people in each of these countries from the specific experiences we were having.

We had an interesting talk with one of the sisters and her husband who told us about some of the courting and marriage customs of Iran. Since most couples were not allowed any privacy while they were courting and therefore didn't really get to know each other, they had two marriages. The first one took place in the home of the woman's parents. They stayed there without sex until the parents decided that they were ready to have the second marriage. In the circumstances, given the lack of privacy beforehand, this seemed an excellent idea as it gave them the chance to see if they were suited without the woman losing her virginity so that she was still marriageable. We had no idea if this was a custom specific to Iran. Her husband told us that he wanted to continue his studies in England so we hoped that we could help him in some way.

On the third full day of our stay 26th March, having organised visas for Afghanistan and bus tickets to Mashhad for 300 rials, we were invited to lunch at the home of the wealthy boyfriend of another of the sisters. It was really interesting to see how opulent this mansion was with all its beautiful tapestries and Persian carpets. We loved the meal too, starting with a vegetable soup then followed by several main dishes including a typical rice dish mixed with beans and saffron, a dish of chicken, one of mutton in a spicy sauce with maize and a lettuce salad of hard boiled eggs, yogurt and parsley. We ended this scrumptious feast with exotic fresh fruit.

Conversation was really interesting, and we came to see that the sister whom we had got to know best was far more of an independent thinker and courageous young woman than we had realised and that she was completely encouraged to be so by her father. Given her free-spirited nature, she felt very unhappy in Iran, frustrated and too different from others to feel understood. She felt she had outgrown her people. She was a good artist and was studying to be an interior designer. We would have been delighted to help her come to London.

We were coming to realise that we had been privileged throughout this journey to meet with some unusually well educated and thinking people in countries where it seemed that education was not available for the majority, especially the women.

In the evening, we drove around looking at architecture with a lively group of their friends, and in the evening returned to the Marine Base and watched an uninspiring western and were given some sandwiches for our journey the following day. The pressure to move on was always with us, as much as anything because we wanted to get to Nepal before the mists and monsoons came and obscured the wonderful mountain views there.

At 5:30 a.m. on Friday 27ᵗʰ March we were at the bus station ready to catch the 6 a.m. bus to Mashhad. We were really sad to say goodbye to our lovely friends but we expected to see them again in a couple of months on our return trip. Unfortunately, events beyond our control were to overtake us and this never happened.

The nineteen hour bus trip was more or less uneventful with little to watch out of the windows, the road at times indistinguishable from the open, dusty barrenness of the surrounding countryside. Occasionally, there were signs of fortified village enclosures to break the monotonous view. However, we were amazed at the kindness of two lorry drivers who invited us to share their meagre meal with them on the bus.

Mud village in Semnan desert en route to Mashhad

There was some trouble in the night after we arrived at Mashad when the taxi driver charged us double the going fare to the hotel and got into a quarrel with another taxi driver and the owner of the hotel we wanted to stay at. As a result, and one and a half hours later, we ended up spending much of the night in the bus company cafe with what seemed like all the homeless of Mashhad, amusing them with lessons in basic English and drawing for them. A policeman then put us in the taxi of the very driver who had taken us to the hotel and made him take us there for free! Either this was an ironic stroke of fate or he had somehow learnt what had happened.

It was now 28th March and, not wanting to spend any more time in Mashhad, we decided to make for the Afghan border. We came to the conclusion that for the most part, the Iranian people were bright but frustrated and that many of them felt unable to channel their creativity and energy into positive and useful actions. This seemed to result in some aggression and interest in money. Amongst the poor and uneducated, every man, woman and child that we had met seemed to be on the make. We couldn't blame them really because they were lively people and needed an outlet. Even though David and I were travelling with relatively little money, few belongings and staying at the simplest of hotels, we knew that we were comparatively well off and privileged compared to most of them.

We caught a bus to the Iranian / Afghan border for 105 rials, but had to change buses in Taybat for an Afghan one. If we had thought the previous buses uncomfortable, they were nothing in comparison to these. They were dirty, falling to pieces and worst of all, the seats had no springs and the roads were uneven and full of holes. It was a slow, extremely uncomfortable ride. The Afghans always seemed to be quarrelling about one thing or another. These quarrels led to the bus often stopping while they tried to sort out the conflicts! As a result, what was a short distance trip from Mashhad to Herat actually took an incredible 15 hours! We then spent ages at the border where efficiency was unheard of. It was now 11:30 p.m. and winter yet again.

A family of Pakistanis had illegally tried to make a pilgrimage to Mecca in Saudi Arabia without money. They had managed to get through Afghanistan but had been stopped at the border. Their passport was out of date and it said they had two children whereas they actually had five! They had tried to alter it with their own handwriting. They were eventually allowed on the bus and a kind Pakistani man paid for their fare and gave them some money. We left some food on the bus for them.

I was glad that they were succeeding in their spiritual journey in spite of not meeting the official requirements, and I wondered what lay behind this need to go to Mecca. I learnt later that it is one of the biggest pilgrimages in the world and that every able-bodied Muslim is expected to go at least once in his life time. It is called the Hajj and is a demonstration of the solidarity of the Muslim people and their submission to God whom they call Allah.

We made friends with this Pakistani man who had helped the family. His name was Rashid. He was a sophisticated man and beautiful to look at. He owned three clothes factories in Pakistan and travelled all over the world selling Pakistani fashions. This year of 1970 was apparently the year of Oriental fashions.

We took a cold but magical and atmospheric ride through the night in a pony cart taxi with him from the bus station and travelled along the rough road. It crossed the barren, Registan Desert and was marked by double rows of pine trees. It was an experience I shall never forget. The sky descended right down to the edge of the desert, illuminated by the most amazing display of stars I have ever seen. The gentle jingling of the pony as it trotted along was juxtaposed by eerie and dissonant sounds of dogs - or was it wolves - howling across the miles and miles of sand. For me, it was one of the peak experiences of the whole trip.

The taxi deposited us at the Park Hotel but it was full so we walked to the 'best' hotel in Herat which was a very modern looking hotel built by the Russians. Our friend treated us to breakfast and we soon discovered that the hotel's sophistication was in appearance only: there was no welcome, no hot water, no lights after 11 pm and no service. The hotel had never been finished! We guessed that the Russian money had run out.

Rashid was also on his way to Kandahar and this proved very helpful to us as not only was he a wealthy and generous man but he also knew what the price of things should be. We were so tired that we missed the 6 a.m. bus which meant that we would have to get a taxi. This would normally have cost 2,000 rupees, but he was able to negotiate the price down to 900, David and I only paying 500 of that. And so we continued our journey across the desert in a taxi: this time of the mechanical type.

Our entertaining taxi driver with his pride and joy: a Russian car

It was a lovely relaxing day with Rashid, the weather hot and sunny. He often talked to the driver because every so often he fell asleep! When awake, he had quite a sense of humour and entertained us by singing love songs! Sometimes we stopped for meals beside the road or for a drink of tea, which was black with lemon. Coffee was thick and extremely strong. Although the scenery was still desolate, there were beautiful colours in the mountains.

We had lunch with a local villager in his mud hut seated crossed-legged on a rug on the earth. They might have thought me rude as I was not able to sit that way. Rashid had warned us that there were strict rules about how to eat, particularly as there were no washing facilities. The meat, which I think was goat, was wrapped and cooked slowly in the hot sand. We each had a small bowl containing four pieces of meat on rice with a few vegetables. It was delicious. We ate with our right hands, knowing that the left was used for toiletry purposes. I couldn't help wondering how they prepared the food with one hand.

Around us there were camels and other animals and occasionally women, completely covered from head to foot and with a rectangle of gauze over their eyes so they could see. We learnt later that this garment is known as a burqa. The men were either bare foot or wearing strange foot wear made of goat skins. On their heads were glittery cloths, over which they sometimes added a turban. They wore tunics mainly over billowy trousers. We didn't know what people they were as there were many different tribes in Afghanistan. The men wanted to watch me riding the camel, so after one of them eventually managed to get it to sit down, I succeeded in climbing onto it with more difficulty than grace it must be said, to take a short, undulating ride side-saddle.

In the desert

The closer we got to Kandahar, the hotter the temperature became, rising to about 90 degrees Fahrenheit (32 degrees Celsius.) In the evening, we had dinner in another village, again in a mud hut and this time, before we started the meal, a villager gave us a bar of soap to wash our hands with while he poured water over them. We ate onion soup followed by a large amount of chicken in rice, but cooked in so much fat that we had trouble getting it off our hands.

A blind man was also seated cross-legged on the mat with us to share the meal. We found him lively and much travelled since his disability allowed him to travel free on the buses and he had used this privilege to travel to several countries. He told us that he wanted a wife from England and hoped to get an operation there. I was beginning to realise that the people we met often thought that we could be their saviours and help them out of whatever trouble they were in and into whatever dreams they had.

Before the Russians built the road through the desert, the journey had apparently taken five days but we arrived in Kandahar at about 9:30 pm and we were happy for Rashid to choose a hotel for us as he'd been there before. It was clean and cosy, and he was so well known by the hotel manager that the same room was always reserved for him. To save us money, they put two more beds in there for us. It struck me as rather odd that I was allowed in the same bedroom as Rashid but we didn't discuss this, and in the event, we all slept really well.

We left Kandahar for Kabul at 6 a.m. the following morning 30th March promising to meet up there with Rashid later. We'd had several conversations with him that had given us ideas about our lives when we returned to England. Although he sold clothes all over the world, he had nowhere for their sale in England. I thought that perhaps I could have an outlet for them in a boutique in Oxford where we would be moving to once we got back, though Rashid would have preferred London. Also, we'd discussed the hospitality of oriental people and had experienced so much of it on our travels that it made us want to be far more hospitable on our return.

It was such an uncomfortable journey but we did enjoy our stop-over for lunch at Gazni where we had a meal and tea for the equivalent of one old shilling each. We would have enjoyed looking around as there were so many wonderful crafts there. I would have liked to buy one of the beautiful silk embroidered sheepskin coats, which had become all the rage among hippies back home.

Through the windows we saw many wandering groups of people with donkeys, camels and sheep. I also found the Afghan trucks fascinating, painted as they were with bright scenes of all kinds. These were mainly romantic in nature: rockets going into the sky, animals and idyllic landscapes and the odd advertisement. There were also short admonitions on the back of the trucks such as 'Use horn and travel safe.'

I fell in love with the muted colours of the scenery and decided that they would make a wonderful colour scheme for our new home: the gold of the ground, the beige, mushroom and browns of the mountains with their purple shadows and the blue of the sky. The majority of villages along the way were in bad repair but as we drew nearer to Kabul, new enclosures had been carefully built out of mud and looked strong.

We arrived in Kabul at about 3:30 pm and went straight to the poste restante to see if there were any letters from our families. Disappointingly there weren't any and we were concerned that we were travelling faster than they realised. We hoped that we wouldn't leave before any letters arrived. We were delighted however to find one from John - our Australian friend from Ibiza, - who had left us a message as we'd hoped to let us know his plans.

We were amazed to discover that he was still in Kabul waiting for some money to come through. As he had given us the name of his hotel we immediately made our way there, excited to be meeting up with him again.

Kabul with the Hindu Kush in the background

We eventually found the hotel which was very grotty indeed and climbed the stairs looking forward to seeing him. We passed a young and somewhat child-like Spanish couple who let us know that there was a heavy drug scene going on in the hotel, centred in John's room.

At the top of the stairs, we did indeed find John in his room, drugged up to the eyeballs from three solid days of smoking marijuana without food. It seemed that he had lost all reason in Herat where he had met up with a French hippie called Jean and had sold his shoes there in order to buy a kilo of hash for $20: a large bag full. He'd been smoking ever since. We took him out of the hotel and the smell of hash in the hopes of getting some sense out of him but he could talk of nothing else and just longed to get back for another smoke. Eventually, we had to let him have his way so we returned and entered the room with him.

There were certainly some strange people there: one of them was a bedraggled English man with long, blonde hair, an Indian accent and dressed in a long robe. He said he had been living in India for two years before returning to Kabul. He was obsessed with how bad the world was and wandered around telling people this. He had no other conversation at all. The Afghan people didn't seem to take any notice of the behaviour of these foreigners as far as we could tell, but I couldn't imagine that they had any respect for them.

We left them to find an evening meal and were glad to find that life was becoming cheaper. We paid 24 afghanis in all for our rice meal with chai (tea). There were 75 afghanis to the dollar at the time.

Back in John's room in the evening, we smoked a chillum – a clay pipe – traditionally used by Sadhus - wandering Hindu monks in India. Various people who'd come from different parts of the world dropped in to join us. There were Arabs, French, Americans, and the Spanish couple we had met on the stairs. Meanwhile, two Syrian Arabs provided some music, one playing the guitar and the other, a stringed instrument. We also ate oranges and local sugary sweets.

David was badly affected by the hashish, and turned white. Even the one inhalation I'd had caused me to be dizzy for a while and we suspected it was extremely strong. I wasn't attracted by this ritual, and I hated seeing John so emotionally addicted to it. It made me feel that perhaps David and I were on a different path from him and that perhaps we shouldn't be together. I felt that people drew experiences into their lives that in some way reflected their inner state of consciousness. Given that we were facing so many unknown and potentially dangerous situations on this trip, I sensed that we needed to be alert. We would have to see what John did now that we had joined him.

The following day 31ˢᵗ March John, Jean, David and I went to the Pakistani Embassy to arrange for road passes and heard that there had been an earthquake in Turkey. We couldn't find out where it was though. Later, we had a very inexpensive Afghan lunch of goodness knows what minced meat and vegetable 'puffs'. John and Jean decided to go back in search of the Spanish couple and continue smoking dope while we strolled around and eventually relaxed on a patch of grass in the sunshine. By the time that we decided to get up and leave, a huge crowd of people were also sitting on the grass around us! It was really amusing. It seemed that their lives were both easier and harder than ours from the extreme simplicity of them. However, sadly, we didn't meet any Afghans who could speak English and tell us anything about their lives.

John and Jean continued to spend the evening with the Spanish couple getting stoned. We spent an hour with a money changer because we had heard that it was possible to double our money in Kabul. The usual rate of exchange on the street for our American dollars was 12.50 Indian rupees to the dollar and eventually, David managed to get 12.63 rupees for them. If we had done this through a bank, the rate would have been 7.5 so we did extremely well. We then met up with Rashid at his clean hotel in the evening and we joined him for a meal. We were so pleased to see his friendly smile. He emanated charm, and to be with him was something of a relief after John and Jean.

He was tired though and soon returned to his hotel. We met the English foursome we had first met in their truck on the Hamah to Kandahar road who were on their way to Kashmir. We chatted with them for a while and arranged for them to see

Rashid's samples with us the following day. The two women were dress designers.

On Wednesday 1ˢᵗ April we met Rashid again for lunch at his hotel and then we were joined by the foursome. The samples were exquisite, though I felt that it was the work in them rather than the styles that made them stand out. I wondered if perhaps the latter was something I would be able to influence so that they would be more attractive to the English fashion industry. The embroidery was done by hand and was so dense that I couldn't imagine how it was ever finished and there were many mirrors included in it. Because labour was so cheap in Pakistan, the garments were also really inexpensive. All of us wanted to buy so many things and we were working out how we could start up a boutique to sell them.

We took Rashid out for a meal at the Khyber Restaurant, which was quite a surprise after the other restaurants we had been to on our trip in that it had a door-man and westernised self-service! After that, we helped Rashid pack up his samples and he surprised and delighted me by giving me one of his older styles which I felt I could easily alter as well as a red, embroidered square of cloth that demonstrated the quality of the work. We hoped to meet up with Rashid in July or August so that we could help him sell his samples. Right now, he was off to Finland via Russia, spending a year in Europe to promote sales and meet up with his many girlfriends. As David put it, he was uncomplicated and happy, rich and unconcerned.

We certainly didn't learn much about life in Pakistan from him in spite of our questions. What he did tell us was that the government took a lot of tax, which could have been annoying to someone like Rashid who earned so much money but he didn't say so. He told us that education was not free, and that although there was a free health service, too many people needed it for it to be effective in any sense of the word. There were alternative health services, all of varying prices. We also heard that a man could see a photo of his future wife but was not allowed to see her in real life except in the most modern of families. He told us that foreigners were not allowed to take photos of the women.

On Thursday 2nd April David and I set off to catch the 8 a.m. bus to Peshawar in Pakistan, wondering if John and Jean would manage to get up after all their smoking. Amazingly they made it to the bus and without the hashish which had apparently gone off. John actually seemed glad that he was now free of the selling game.

We had been expecting an interesting and spectacular trip on this journey but nothing like as impressive as it actually turned out to be. The weather was perfect and the scenery breathtaking. The bus took a route through the Kabul Gorge, a dramatically beautiful, deep gorge, with glittering rock formations and the river swirling and falling. At one point, the road doubled back on itself twice to fall to the bottom of the gorge. The walls were a thousand feet high on either side, vast and craggy with a few trees on grassy patches by the river bank. It was actually an incredibly dangerous road but I would not have missed that experience for the world.

Then the valley widened out into lush, green paddies, still lakes and trees fully out in the new leaves of spring. I couldn't believe how many different kinds of trees there were and so many in blossom. The Hindu Kush Mountains were dark with mystery, snow lying on the distant peaks. I hadn't been ready for such a vision. We had always been told that it was the Khyber Pass that was breathtaking and we hadn't yet reached it.

As we began to lose altitude, the temperature rose. We were most surprised by the town of Jalalabad, though it seems I was too tired to write why this was. The trees and shrubs there continued in all their beautiful variety and we should have loved to spend time there but the bus did not stop.

We rattled off into the night with our luggage on our knees in case we fell asleep. I could not continue to keep my eyes open at all and I actually slept through our journey through the Khyber Pass! David assured me that it was nothing in comparison with the previous gorge and valley, but I shall never know. Apparently, along the paths were a number of mud walled fortified houses and all the men carried guns. What had impressed him though was the construction of the railway line over the Khyber. He said there had been a spectacular view of it looking down from the highest point into the Pakistani Plain.

As soon as we arrived at the Afghanistan / Pakistan border we noticed the new heat which was around 95 degrees Fahrenheit (35 Celsius) and the strong smell of jasmine blossom. We got through without difficulty and arrived in Peshawar at about 4.30 pm.

A market street in *Peshawar. John and Jean can be seen to the right of the picture.*

Later, we hired an old chap with his 'taxi' which was a horse-drawn wagon, to take us around the town. It was unexpectedly lovely with its tree-lined avenues and fragrant blossoms. The evening air was balmy. The horse trotted round gently, but even so, the people on foot seemed to walk too close to it for comfort. The driver took us round the bazaar and waited for us while we looked round the jewellery stalls, shafts of sunlight glinting through the buildings.

While he waited, we walked a little way into the city where we saw both the rich and penniless, the educated and the illiterate. There were still signs of the previous British civilisation, especially in the names such as, 'The Prince of Wales Cafe' and 'The Mall'. We also found it in the polite, somewhat deferential service we received later while we had a curry. Then we continued our relaxed ride through the night.

Soon we were involved in an experience which seemed more like an excerpt from a film than reality. It was clear that our driver had more than one business concern as he offered to sell us some hashish. Jean was very interested since he and John no longer had any. It was so 'cloak and dagger', with Jean insisting on sampling it while the driver stopped every so often near a tree to give him cover while he looked out for police. At the time I was frightened as I was aware that such a discovery by the police could mean a dangerous end to our journey. In the later safety of retrospection, it was hilarious!

Jean was completely hooked by hashish, smoking it at every opportunity, even before breakfast. The friends with whom he had originally left France had all become ill and had returned home. He was practically out of money and did not want to go back as he had been involved in the 1968 student riots against the government. He had also been a dealer there. He knew that he would be taking the hashish through the Pakistan / India border and yet he still bought another huge kilo bar from our driver. His rationale was that he could only survive if he had the hashish to sell. Eventually, the deal was sealed for $11.

We had been told by other overland travellers about the danger of crossing the border with drugs. In particular, we had learnt that there was no chance of getting past the Indian woman who worked as a customs official there. Many people had been imprisoned by her and we understood that we would suffer terribly in an Indian prison where it was said that we would languish forever. It was with a heavy heart that I caught the 8.50 night express bus to Lahore.

We arrived at dawn on 3rd April and I hadn't slept a wink. David hadn't done much better: we were too nervous about going through the border with Jean and his bar of hash. Getting out of the bus, we were surrounded by men who couldn't take their eyes off me. To escape their stares while we waited for the bus to the border, we walked around the typically wide, tree lined streets, enjoying the sights, and were blown away by the beautiful pre-historic looking water buffalo that were pulling the carts. These beasts looked better cared for than the people though they were certainly expected to work hard in exchange for their care and we saw one impossibly huge load being pulled by three of them.

Soon we were on a local bus heading for the border and I wondered if this was the end both of our trip and our freedom. It seems strange now to think that we didn't even consider travelling separately from John and Jean. It is true that we were very fond of John and had shared so much with him already that I suppose we felt we were in this experience together, come what may.

I was so tired and anxious that I could not participate in the conversation that was going on between David, John, Jean and a Pakistani graduate in economics who invited us to stay with him in Islamabad on our return journey. He had also promised that he would take us to Kashmir, renowned for its beauty and which we had been contemplating going to.

The inevitable time to face customs arrived. Jean had hidden the hashish in his pants but there was no turning back now and some force other than my own will propelled me forward. As we neared the hut which was the Pakistani customs office, a large piece fell down his trousers on to the ground near some officials. I seemed to stop breathing and my heart thumped in my ears. Amazingly luck was on our side and their attention elsewhere so we had no trouble getting through. All we could do at this stage was to pray that it wouldn't be the woman customs official on the Indian side.

As we approached the Indian border hut my heart sank for it was indeed this woman on duty. She looked at us and announced that she knew that we had 'shit' on us and told us that it would be better for us if we owned up. We didn't believe it for a minute and were all terrified. Time seemed to stop. I felt sick and I thought Jean was going to cry hysterically.

Suddenly, John began to take all her attention by goading her and then suggesting that perhaps she was right and he was carrying 'shit'. Eventually he suggested she should indeed search him. She asked him why he was trembling. She hesitated for a moment and then started the search.

As we stood watching with our hearts in our mouths, she looked through his bag carefully. Then she unrolled his sleeping bag and felt for the bar. Finally, she searched his person, and of course, couldn't find anything. As she finished, we thought she was about to search Jean and I felt hysterical and watched in terror as I saw Jean touch himself where the drugs were hidden. Didn't he realise he was drawing her attention to himself? She asked Jean to bring his bag over, and our hearts sank. It looked as though we were done for.

What she did next was completely unexpected. Instead of searching either his bag or his person, she gave us a long lecture on bringing hash into India which she told us could have put us into prison when we should be out enjoying ourselves. She also surprised me by saying that it was okay to smoke a bit and to let that be enough. We couldn't believe that she was going to let us go.

We walked across the border into India to freedom and what was to be the most complex country we had ever visited. In a somewhat dazed state, we had a cool drink and then caught a horse taxi cart to the railway station at Ferozepore.

I sat back and began to feel my body relax. I felt I was in some kind of wonderland: everything was so radiant and beautiful, shimmering with light and heat. The grass and leaves were lusciously green; fabulous cream-coloured cows with large deer-like heads were roaming around the roads, and green parakeets and other beautiful birds with unfamiliar songs flew amongst the many kinds of trees, some of which had exotic blossoms and hypnotic scents. The heat was intense but we were sheltered in the wagon and there was a gentle breeze.

Smiling Indians with large white teeth ambled around, and suddenly, our driver decided to race another driver and now we were being thrown around the open wagon! It was as though we had somehow passed a test and been given the key that opens the portal to a strange paradise where the usual rules no longer apply. Once the driver stopped racing we couldn't believe our eyes when he rolled up a joint to share with us, and then a little later, got out a chillum for us to share. The irony of this situation did not escape me and I decided to try it. I did become a little stoned but I really felt that the whole amazing experience was at least equal to being stoned without the need for a drug to give me heightened awareness.

We had planned to push on to Delhi straight away but we found it so difficult to arrange for second class train tickets with sleeping accommodation that we nearly decided to stay in Ferozapore. We had no idea at this point that obtaining travel tickets anywhere in India was always going to require exertions of marathon proportions.

After some discussion, we decided to travel first class for some privacy and rest as we were exhausted so we settled down on the platform to wait for the night train. When the train rolled in, David was delighted to see steam engines again with all the remembered sounds and smells of our childhood. Once on the train though we were disappointed with the first class accommodation as we had received so little for so much extra money: the beds were very hard and there was no bedding and no bar.

Sleep was not that easy to come by. We got into conversation with a Canadian dealer who had just spent five weeks in a Pakistani prison for carrying twelve kilos of hash. He said that someone had informed on him. He'd paid the maximum fine or he would have stayed in prison for five years. He too had just gone through customs with the same Indian woman who apparently had wept. She had told him how unhappy and how rich she was from all the bribes she took, he added. She said she could always tell when someone was carrying shit and had caught many travellers. He warned Jean that many people were caught dealing drugs in Delhi, which is where Jean was planning to sell his, and that the best thing to do was to post it, especially to Holland. Someone he had met had just managed to get 100 kilos into Holland hidden in furniture. He suggested the other possibility for Jean was to buy a chess set in which to hide it.

For David and me, this conversation was unnerving. However, we did manage to get some sleep eventually, though Jean woke us up in the early hours. We were due to arrive in Delhi at 6:15 a.m. but at 3:15 he woke and asked John if there was time to smoke a chillum!

On Saturday 4th April we arrived in Delhi, very tired. It was strange to see how architecturally Victorian the station looked but all such familiarities disappeared as soon as we left the station and were assailed by beggars. One of them thrust the stump of his lost arm in our faces. A woman kept clutching at my legs and making prayers on my feet. It elicited many confusing emotions from me. We had been warned not to give the beggars anything or we would draw such crowds to us that we would not be able to move but it was difficult not to feel concern.

We walked for miles to the Hindu Birla Mandir Temple where we hoped to stay. We passed many dead bodies under blankets on the pavement. We had been told that if no one had removed them by the evening, they were taken away in a cart to be cremated. Cows wandered across the road aimlessly, holding up the traffic. The roads were spacious and lined with trees and bordered by huge mansions with lovely gardens, formerly owned by the British.

We were exhausted and dripping with sweat when we eventually reached the temple, only to discover that the rooms for visitors were full! We were told to return early on Monday with a letter of introduction from the British Embassy.

Saturday was not a good time to arrive in Delhi with the embassies shut and the shops closed the following day. We still needed somewhere to stay but I was running out of energy to continue walking in this heat. Eventually, Jean and I rested in a hotel called the Ceylon Rest Home while David and John went looking for somewhere to stay.

John had been to Delhi a couple of years before and told us that the prices had risen considerably since then. All that they were able to get now for 5 rupees a head was one room to share between the four of us in a bazaar area. The hotel they eventually found was called Neelam Hotel in the Paharganj main bazaar.

Meanwhile, I stayed in the grounds and exchanged spiritual ideas with the manager who was interested in mine and why we were travelling. I communicated my thinking with him using spiritual, scientific terms while he tended to express his own ideas in parables. For instance, he said that the river always seemed to be moving and changing, and yet it was the bubbles that broke away from it while the river stayed the same. Although we communicated our sense of the Divine and its expression as the universe in a completely different way, we certainly understood each other. When David returned, the manager told him in his strong Indian accent that he had enjoyed talking to me and, 'She has much wisdom, but no shape!' I like to think that this spoilt compliment was because he couldn't see past my loose brown Syrian top that disguised my curves!

We wandered round the bazaar in the evening, and I was rather upset when children threw stones at us, often succeeding in hitting us. A passing Sikh took pity on us. He apologised for the behaviour of the children and offered us a cup of tea. We were interested to know the difference between Sikhs and Hindus. He told us that there was little difference but that historically, the Sikhs were the fighters. It was they who, 400 years ago, had fought the Moguls who had invaded India and tried to impose the Muslim religion.

He said that the Sikhs were now questioning aspects of their own religion as some of the commandments were outdated. For example, one commandment was that every Sikh should carry a sword. The reason for their long hair which they covered in a turban was so that during an invasion they would be able to be distinguished from the Muslims in battle. He also told us that there were several hundred different languages in India, which created complete disunity. It seemed to me that however we judged the British legacy in India, they had at least done the Indians a favour in introducing English.

On the way back to the hostel, the Sikh shot us a line, which made me question his friendliness towards us. He said that we could make some money by 'losing' our travellers' cheques for so many rupees and then the banks would offer us new cheques. I didn't like the sound of this, and although they were non-committal, John and David said they would meet him the following night.

Sunday 5th April was a real scorcher and we could do little more than laze around for much of the day. We started off in the grounds of the Ceylon Rest House sheltering under a huge tree. We were soon surrounded by young boys who would not leave us alone, constantly asking us questions and presenting us with flowers and cigarettes. One boy offered David 20 rupees for his watch.

There was also a man there sitting cross-legged on the ground who kept making stupid faces and who directed his strange smiles at John. I think he was smitten with him and he followed us back to our hotel. He suggested we go to the cinema with him but when we got there we discovered that it was not the programme we had been told about and it was too expensive at 70 rupees each. We noticed that going to the cinema was a popular pastime there and that many of the people looked very wealthy.

We spent some time in a tea shop watching passers-by but could hardly breathe in the heat. It was fascinating for us to see people who often looked strange to us for they were not to be seen in England at the time. We thought the women were beautiful in their long, colourful saris but we found the Sikh adolescent boys strange to look at with their long hair tied up in a bun and wisps of hair escaping from what looked like a white scarf tied round it. I also enjoyed seeing the clothes of the Sikh women which consisted of a long, loose-fitting tunic over a billowy pair of trousers called a Salwaar Kameez.

In the evening, we had planned to go to the Red Fort and watch the 'Son et Lumières' but by the time we got there it was all over. On the way there, we unfortunately bumped into the Sikh who had proposed the financial deal to us and which even John had decided not to participate in. The heat seemed to make us indecisive and we spent the evening with him in the grounds of a large Hindu temple, sitting under the spray of some green water. We weren't drawn to him and his hard business ways. He told us he planned to go to London and wanted to meet us there so we could fix him up with a woman. He was fascinated by our sexually free way of life and wanted to find out for himself.

He told us about the caste system which he said still existed and that people usually married into their own caste. He said the system originated when the Hindu king ordained that people should be divided up according to what sort of job they were suited to.

Brahmans were at the top and were the religious teachers. He said that the Sikhs came next, and these were the fighters. However, we learnt later that defence was only one part of this caste's possible occupation which also included other kinds of public service such as administration and maintenance of law and order. Then came the business men, and at the bottom were the untouchables who were the road sweepers. It was clear to me that Sikhs were also business men nowadays. I also wanted to understand more about what it meant to be 'an untouchable' in this day and age, but he told me simply that there was nothing to be gained from contact with them.

It seemed amazing to us that a whole group of people could still be seen as so different from everyone else that they were excluded and isolated and thought to pollute others somehow by their very touch. How terrible to be born an untouchable! While in discussion with this man we were surrounded yet again by a group of energetic young Sikhs, and we left. I felt relieved that John had decided not to enter into any business deals.

The following day 6th April we got the necessary letters of introduction from our embassy to get into the Birla Hindu Temple and then walked on to the French Embassy for Jean's letter. Back at the temple, we discovered to our dismay that it was still full. Although exhausted from walking so far in the heat, David and I set off for the Post Office near Connaught Place which was the commercial hub of New Delhi. On the way there, we caught sight of the parliament buildings which were very grand and Indo-classic in style. However, I was alarmed to see red stained walls and red splotches on the roads, thinking that it was blood. However, we learnt later that it was the digestive – paan, made from betal nut that the Indians chewed after meals and then spat out. I had also been taken aback by the fact that there was chilli in absolutely everything, including the fruit salads. Was it addictive, I wondered?

After that, we walked to the hospital for our second cholera inoculation. There was a very long queue but we managed somehow to make for the front of it and received prompt attention. The nurse gave us four times the amount that we had had for the first injections. We became feverish with a very high temperature and our injected arms were agony. All afternoon and evening we lay in our room in the Neelam Hotel and meanwhile, a great drama unfolded around us.

John told us that he had met a traveller who said he was interested in buying hashish, and Jean had decided to sell him some. It involved several meetings with John and Jean: one in a park where this and another man had sampled the quality of it and told him it was bad quality and that he would only pay twice what Jean had paid. We were worried about John involving himself in all this as he didn't seem to realise that dealing in drugs was a serious matter but Jean said he couldn't manage on his own and John had a soft heart.

That evening, a man who worked there and who had befriended us, came and told us that the men whom John and Jean were meeting were actually police pimps; that they would buy the shit and then inform on them, which is what they had done to some Europeans who had stayed at the hotel previously. He told us that now that they knew this at the hotel, neither of the two men were allowed to enter it and that we should have no dealings with them.

Unfortunately, when this kind employee was nowhere in sight, another hotel employee brought both men up to our room which meant that they could see all of us. We realised then that David and I had also been implicated in this dangerous situation, and I was so thankful when David issued an ultimatum to Jean: he must either get rid of the hashish or separate from us. We were so ill though that John had to deal with it. He told Jean to put the block of hashish into a jacket and then took him away from the hotel to leave it in a locker in a left luggage office. While they were gone, David and I made the decision to separate from Jean anyway, whatever John decided.

By Tuesday 7ᵗʰ April, although we had still not recovered and I had a high temperature, David, John and I managed to get a room at the Birla Mandir Temple. It was plain and simple and open to the elements but amazingly it was free, and we felt we were very privileged to be in such a place. We had to get accustomed to the chanting though as it never ceased.

A scribe in the Birla Mandir Temple in Delhi

We thought that now, with Jean and his hashish elsewhere, we could relax. But we were wrong. The drama continued to unfold around us, drawing us in, and although David and I had collapsed on our mattresses, there was to be no peace for us.

This time it was John, not Jean, who was attracting the events to us. When he returned from his outing, he was very excited and said that he had got a wonderful proposition for us. He told us that he had met an Indian who planned to tour Europe but wasn't allowed travellers cheques and only a very small allowance. For that reason, he would be prepared to give us dollars at a very good rate for any travellers cheques we would sell him and that we could go to the bank to determine that the dollars were genuine.

John decided he was definitely game to do this, particularly as he had also met a New Zealander who said he had done that very thing yesterday and intended to change $900 more. It seemed to be such a genuine deal as well as profitable that we gave John our travellers' cheques too. We weren't in any state to go with him and check these people out. Neither were we in any state to make such a decision but David at least had the forethought to tell John that he should not part with the cheques until he had the dollars in his hand.

Half an hour later, John returned in a panic. We could hardly believe it when he told us that he had done something incredibly stupid. He had handed over every single one of our cheques, - all $1400 worth of them to the New Zealander, had watched him go into the bank, waited outside and then had realised that this man was not going to be coming back! He had obviously gone out a back way.

We were in a terrible state of shock. All our money was gone. Our travels were going to be at an end without the means to get home. We just couldn't believe that John could have done such a stupid thing.

Luckily, David was by now feeling much better and able to think more clearly. He and John thought that we could be issued with new travellers cheques if we got to American Express in time to cancel the others that had been stolen. Thank God we had recorded the numbers of these. In a way, it was a blessing that I was too ill to be involved because I was quite unable to lie about things which they were going to have to do if we stood any chance of getting our cheques re-issued. I waited with a state of feverish panic for many hours for their return.

When they eventually got back, I couldn't believe our luck to learn that we would eventually get the cheques re-issued. But it had not been easy, and they had needed the endurance of a marathon runner and the patience of saint. David and John had started off at the American Embassy where they were told that they needed a signed copy of their statement by the police before anything could be done. They rushed off to the nearest police station and had been frustrated and surprised at how the police had behaved. Not one was prepared to take their statement. However, a constable accompanied them to two more police stations where the same indifference existed. Was this some kind of punishment or game?

Apparently, many of the police they met were lying around half-naked doing nothing at all. David and John had spotted a list up on the wall of one station showing the number of police who had been suspended. It was 10 percent! Finally, at the fourth station, one of the policemen had agreed to sign their statement.

They returned to the American Embassy with a copy of their signed, sealed statement, assuming that they had completed everything necessary. This was not to be and they spent a long time filling out many forms. Still this was not sufficient and there was a lot more energy to be expended before they reached the finishing line. They were informed that they now needed to get a 5 rupee stamp from the Notary. How interesting that they hadn't been told this on their first visit there! What was more, they needed to complete all this by the end of the day or they wouldn't be able to stop the travellers cheques going through. They set off yet again, obtained the stamp and just managed to return to the embassy before it closed at 5:00 p.m.. They realised that their endeavours had been worth it when the official told them they should have the cheques in a few days.

We had been so stupid and so naive! We were also beginning to realise that many Indians seemed to be involved in some kind of racket. The New Zealander had joined forces with one of them to outwit unwary travellers. He himself had probably been tricked in the same way originally and then could not survive without involving himself in a similar trick. It has often struck me since that it only takes a moment for a wrong decision which can alter our whole life and even ruin it. We had been so lucky not to be one of those people. In fact, trusting people was becoming problematic. The next time we were approached by a man with a possible scam we didn't give him the time of day, in spite of his artfully if somewhat naively-worded suggestion: 'I make collection of foreign coins; not for personal profit but to learn about the customs of other countries!'

On Wednesday 8th April, with calm restored, we just walked around, taking in the atmosphere and newness of India. There was so much to experience and it completely bombarded our senses. I was also having difficulty in finding the appetite to eat anything because of the heat which had risen from 100 to 104 degrees Fahrenheit (about 38 to 40 degrees Celsius.) David insisted that I force down one small meal a day at least. Drinking was also a problem. We had been warned at the Embassy that the water was not safe here but our mouths were always dry. Every time we stopped at a cafe, we were each brought a glass of ice-cold water, torturing us by its presence. There was neither bottled water then nor any non-fizzy drink. We were ordering iced coffee and lassi, a yogurt drink, but later realised that these had probably been made from unboiled water.

I had found a letter waiting for me at the India High Commission from my brother Richard and had been surprised to learn that there was snow in England. It seemed rather desirable in the overheated state I was in. In the road where the Nepalese Embassy was, we bumped into both Jean and also the quiet, smiling Spanish couple we had first met in Kabul. They were all planning to go to Nepal so we figured we would be seeing them again there. Jean told us that his hash had gone bad.

I met a fortune teller on the street who told me that 1969 had been a bad year for me but that 1970 and 1971 would be good, especially the next six months, and in particular, June. She told me that I would not find what I was searching for in India and would soon leave but would find it elsewhere; that my husband loved only me and I had two other men who loved me in secret, their names beginning with J and W. I would also receive 30,000 rupees. I was very sceptical about fortune tellers and particularly this one, but we would see.

While we were walking around the grounds of the temple, something happened that makes me blush just to think of it: a woman approached me and told me that I was obscene to be walking round in a petticoat! She asked me how I would react to a woman walking down the King's Road in Chelsea in a petticoat. I was so shocked and embarrassed. I had no idea that the long, thick cotton skirt that I'd purchased in Delhi in place of my winter trousers was a petticoat to go under saris. I became very self-conscious, even though the skirt was neither transparent nor seductive.

Later, my mood improved after meeting a sincere young graduate who had no business plan for us, was religious and who told us about the Hindu religion. He said that there were two main paths: the way of what he referred to as the mendicant and the way of the active man. The former lived in the jungles and ate berries and fruit and whatever he could find there. His way was the way of renunciation and meditation. This is apparently what the Buddhists had reacted against because they had seen it as a form of escapism. He said that, like Buddhists, both the mendicant and the active man wished to reach the state of Nirvana. The active man had to do good deeds, with good motives and without thought of the results of his deeds to prevent pride. This way was considered much more difficult than the way of the mendicant.

He told us that there were many gods, known as lords, who could all be worshipped but there was only one God. It seemed that these gods provided focus for specific prayers, and I could see the attraction of such an idea. He said there were eighty four different castes with thousands of sub castes. They believed in the re-incarnation of their souls and that badness would be punished at some point, whether in this life or the next. Right thinking was fundamental to this. The cow was sacred because it was seen as a mother giving milk to the whole of humanity.

He added that people in the countryside had large families based on their belief that there would be more children finding employment and therefore able to give them their wages. However, in practice, neither of these things tended to happen so they were underfed. He surprised us by saying that the women of India were better qualified than the men, and we wondered how that was happening. He was planning to go to England to study business management, but he did not ask us to do anything for him.

The following morning 9th April, for some reason, perhaps the heat, I just felt defeated and wanting to cry. David and John let me stay in the air-conditioned tourist office for most of the day while they did all the hard work involved in recovering our travellers cheques. I should imagine that the additional problem of an emotional woman with them would have been the final straw in any case. They arrived back eventually with all the travellers cheques and told me that they had met five other travellers who had been tricked by the same Indian and that the New Zealander had indeed also been in on the scam.

Later in the afternoon, David and I were taken aback to meet a New Zealander in the tourist office. He seemed a straight-forward enough chap and didn't seem to fit John's description of him so we told him about his compatriot. When we later met John and described him, he said that it sounded just like the one who'd tricked him. If I had found out for sure, I don't think that I would ever have trusted my judgement of another person's character again. Yet trust is such an important thing in life. I was concerned not to lose it as I felt that trust and openness went hand-in-hand and were necessary for a rich experience of life. Since we'd arrived in India, we seemed to be getting a crash course in wising up to the ways of the world. We needed to be more alert but this damned heat made it so difficult. Delhi was a most frustrating and exhausting place!

We spent Friday 10th April from 12 a.m. to 6 p.m. simply trying to get train tickets with concessions and seat reservations from Northern Railways. It entailed a lot of form filling and being sent to various departments in completely different parts of the city. We could not find a single official who was willing to make the decision to issue us with the tickets. Ultimately, when someone did sell us tickets, he short-changed us and we had to go through yet another bureaucratic rigmarole to get our money back! As David said, only the strong and patient could cope with this madness.

Yes, the British helped the Indians find some sense of unity through teaching them one language and building a wonderful railway, but the Indian mind did not seem able to grasp the point of the bureaucracy that the British left behind them. But does bureaucracy serve anyone? Even in England it tends to exceed its brief, serving itself rather than what it is set up to serve.

In the evening we hung around with various Indian men and learnt more about their religious and social customs. One thing that I found interesting was that it was the custom for parents to choose whom their children would marry, yet in Delhi at least 60 percent of young people were apparently making their own choice of a marriage partner. In spite of this, the dowry continued to be given by the woman's family to the man's. They told us that there was little disobedience by Indian children because they felt so loved and families were so close. Children felt homesick if they left home. That might well have been true for middle class Indians, but although it sounded wonderful, I felt that the other side of that coin was a huge pressure to conform.

Because of the experiences we had had in Delhi we did not feel able to accept an invitation to stay with one of the men. It had been a fascinating but hugely frustrating six days, and we were pleased to be moving on the following day. All the images and experiences had battered and overwhelmed us: extremes of heat, of beauty and ugliness, the smell of urine on the walls, the disorganisation, the mad bureaucracy, the noise, the endless beggars, scooter taxis, lassie drinks, lollies and coca cola, the cadgers and roaming swindlers.

So on Saturday 11th April we boarded the train to Agra with surprising ease at 7:35 a.m. and we even had seats. I was conscious that it was my mother's birthday, though sadly she was no longer alive. I was still crying when I thought of her, even though she had died of lupus when I was twenty five, eighteen months earlier. Little did I know then, sitting on this train in India, just how much significance this event was going to have on the rest of my complex life. Her illness and subsequent death had made a deep impact on me, haunting me for decades to come.

It was also to be the event that was pivotal in spurring me on to make sense of this life and to find out who I really was. To lose a mother is significant in anyone's life and at any age and we expect to grieve. But something in me had frozen at the moment when the dreaded announcement came from St Mary's Hospital in Praed Street that she was dead. A neighbour in my father's house at the time had held out her arms to me and I could not succumb.

I let my thoughts drift to the landscape flashing by. It was flat with fields of golden corn being slowly cut by the hands of women reapers, ox-drawn carts parked nearby ready to take the sheaves away. Much of the land was scrub: dry and not tillable. I could also see tropical palm trees, the straw huts of the villages, groups of people resting in the shade of other unknown trees and cows roaming around. The bird life was different too. There were some very large heron-like birds by the river, some as big as children, with long legs and pink beaks.

After three hours, we arrived in Agra, but we were finding the heat so difficult that it was even hard to think about going to the Taj Mahal, one of the wonders of the world. Such extreme heat must control how people lived and felt about their lives. We were realising how important comfort was when we didn't have it! However, we took a taxi to the Red Fort which was a celebrated and fine piece of ancient Mughal architecture made from red sandstone. David especially appreciated its majesty and the sophistication of the people who built it. He described it as 'massive, complicated and delicate' combining as it did 'fortification and habitation in a happy space on a human scale.'

We also visited four of the local shops to see the range of local crafts and saw some beautiful things: various objects made of marble and inlaid with semi-precious stones and mother of pearl in the manner of the Taj Mahal; also carved, scented sandalwood and ivory, precious stones and fine Kashmiri carpets. Unlike the usual tourists, we always had to resist purchasing the things that we fell in love with.

Luckily, after the window shopping we did go on to the remarkable Taj Mahal which, though built by a Mughul emperor in the seventeenth century, was of course made from white marble rather than the usual red sandstone and was inlaid with semi-precious stones. It had such a pleasing symmetry. It was indeed a beautiful piece of architecture in every way and satisfied something deep in our souls. It was cool in the sanctuary with a low light and a humming noise which made for a very special, sacred atmosphere. Although David found this thought of mine fanciful, I suggested that the striking contrast of the Red Fort and the Taj Mahal was a particular expression of masculine and feminine architecture; the former standing for physical strength, power and dominance, and the latter for love, delicacy and purity.

We understood that it had been built as a mausoleum by the emperor in loving memory of his favourite wife Mumtaz who had died in child birth. It was also rumoured that the emperor had ordered the architect to be killed so that he could never again build anything of such exquisite beauty. The grounds were beautiful too, and although formal in their design which I normally didn't enjoy, they were in perfect keeping with the symmetry of the building and had the added attraction of huge butterflies, exotic birds, fountains and trees. We lay on thick grass and watched the sky, the trees and the birds as evening began to take over from afternoon, and saw that the Taj took on a different and more mysterious hue in the sunset.

We returned to Agra city by cycle rickshaw. As usual, I felt uncomfortable for the two of us to be transported around by one man straining in the heat. We had a good meal and then caught the train to Tundla junction where we met an Israeli and heard a different side to the account of the Israel / Arab conflict. He told us that the Israelis were prepared to fight to the death. He added that they knew they could easily win the war because they were a far more cultured people than the Arabs. However, America was not prepared for that to happen, so Israel stated that she only wanted to keep the Arabs under control and make peace with a gradual removal of her troops from strategic points.

He also told us that their other concessions were that they were prepared to give back most of the land they had gained in 1967 during the Six Day War. They would also take back some of the Palestinian refugees. He said that to have a coalition between Israelis and Arabs was simply not feasible when they had been such enemies. He added that the Israelis felt that this land was theirs by right, not simply through the historical fact of its existence for them 2000 years ago but because since then, it had never left their minds and hearts however much they had been persecuted.

He was aware of America's interest in keeping the Suez Canal open and in the oil of the region. However, in answer to my questions, he did not seem to think that the war would ever take on the proportions of the Vietnam War with the USA and Russia involved. He explained that this was because Russia was not involved in the ideology of the Arabs in the way she had been with the North Vietnamese against South Vietnam and the Americans where ideology had been at stake.

He added that the Israelis had paid the USA for their weaponry but the Egyptians had mortgaged themselves up to the hilt for the next twenty years with the aid they had received from Russia. He felt there was no peaceful solution while the Arabs remained so backward, and that the war was taking all their resources and efforts so that there was none left for making progress anyway. He reckoned that in two or three years' time, there would be another war and that all that Israel could do in the meantime was to keep back the Arab forces. He predicted that peace would come in another forty years or so.

On Sunday 12ᵗʰ April we boarded the train to Benares, now known as Varanasi, travelling third class with three tier sleepers. It is the most sacred city in India. We travelled through a landscape that was flat and parched by the scorching sun. We saw occasional mud villages with poverty-stricken people, cows and children bathing in muddy pools. Meanwhile, we talked to the other passengers. The Indians were finding the heat as difficult as we were. They said that it was the hottest time of the year anyway, that this year it was particularly extreme and that many people had already died.

The man opposite educated us in the ways of the Hindu Ashram System. He told us that a man's life is divided into four stages: Brahricharya, which is a period of learning, and from puberty, a period of sexual abstinence till he is twenty five years old before he marries; Garhastha, which is from then until the age of fifty when he settles down to produce children; then follows the phase of Vanaprastha, which is from fifty until he is seventy five years old during which time he keeps aloof from his wife. Then finally, Sannyasa, which is from seventy five until he dies and during which period he should dedicate his life to God.

He asked us in his strong Indian accent, as so many Indians had before him, 'How many children do you have?' and 'What is the aim and purpose of your visit?' I can't remember now what either David or I replied to the latter. I suppose I did not feel like talking about my spiritual ideas and apart from that, David and I were not people of many aims and purposes during this journey other than to have more experience of life, to see more of the world and learn more of its ways. Perhaps the Indians we met were finding it hard to imagine why anyone from England would wish to travel around India in the uncomfortable way that we were on a shoestring.

We arrived in Benares at 1:30 pm, found the nearest hotel and took a much needed shower. Trains pulled by steam engines were wonderful but because of the necessity to keep the windows open, they always left us covered in soot! Then we lay on the bed until it was nearly dark and we hoped, less hot. Once somewhat refreshed, we set out to explore this town. However, the heat was unbelievable. The only time I had ever experienced heat like this was whenever I had opened the oven door, but here, the door could not be shut. The buildings had sucked up the heat of the day and then breathed it out at night, enveloping us in a cruel embrace. We could hardly put one foot forward after the other. The walk to the Ganges seemed to go on forever.

There were hundreds of people milling around and we knew that they came from all over India to be purified or healed or perhaps to die. There were also cows, rickshaws and one or two cars. At last we arrived at the two sign posts announcing the nearness of the Ganges, but I was horrified by them. One warned us to take care of all our possessions from the thieves. As I read the second one, I became increasingly uneasy with each stipulation:

Do not photograph the beggars.
Do not photograph the paupers.
Do not photograph the lepers.
Do not photograph the burning ghats.
Do not photograph the dead bodies.

We wandered down the steps to the sacred river and we were relieved to be away from the heat of the buildings. If David felt anxious, he did not give it away but I was becoming increasingly worried with all the crowds that I would be touched by lepers, catch leprosy myself and then my limbs would fall off, which was the prevalent belief about leprosy in those days. I had also read a French love story about a leper colony and been deeply moved and disturbed by it. I steeled myself for the sights I would see.

Again, it was an assault on the senses. All along the Ganges by the ghats and the little temples that people had erected to various gods, there were people either lying or sitting or busy with one ritual or another; different noises filled the air: some people were chanting, some shouting. Some were banging drums or sounding horns; bells rang out and different strains of music came from both sides of the river which were lit by a line of lamps. There were many people trying to sell things. The air was thick with gnats and the smell of incense.

My anxiety subsided a little when we took a boat out into the river and talked to some Indian post graduates about the experience. As we moved silently and slowly down the Ganges in the dusk, we could see other boats moving soundlessly from ghat to ghat, rows of bobbing candles, the outline of buildings and all the shadowy human activity at the water's edge. Some of the Ghats had fires burning ready for the bodies to be burnt. People were preparing themselves for their own personal ceremonies at the little altars, mixing up the red paste-like substance to paint jewel like dots on their foreheads, winding cloth around themselves and offering flowers and fruit to the gods. The water rippled with the different colours from the reflections.

However, in spite of this heady potpourri of impressions, the experience continued to challenge me. I was horrified to learn that the bodies were not all burnt and that it was the very ones that we would expect to be burnt: of those who had died from cholera and smallpox, that were put into the Ganges. Some Hindus were drinking from the river, and of course this water from the Ganges was then used as the town's water supply! We decided that we would no longer drink the lassi made from water, yogurt and cane sugar that was sold by so many of the street sellers as a thirst-quenching drink.

We returned to the hotel, and dealt with yet another attempt by the staff to diddle us from some money. Even the Indian guests who had accepted drinks from us did not return the favour. The contrast of our experience in this part of India with Arab countries was surprising to us at the time. We were shocked by how so many Indians had been inhospitable for the most part compared to the Arabs whom we had met, many of them Muslim. From our limited western knowledge of religions, we had considered Hinduism to be very spiritual. Presumably, had we chosen to go only to Ashrams and to be in the presence of Gurus, we would have had a very different experience. Perhaps also it would be different in other parts of India.

There seemed to be a sort of insensitivity and lack of care towards others, though I suspected that it could also come from their belief in fatalism. Even the highly educated post graduates on the river had taken the boat within hearing distance of where some hippies were living in their own boat and had spoken about them in loud voices. It was difficult to imagine how they would ever help the poor and the beggars when they thought that the kind of life they were leading was as a result of bad behaviour in a previous life.

There was also the apathy and exasperation that resulted from the private battle with the sadistic heat that each person was in, which meant that to move a hand, a leg or even to speak was a challenge. Connected to the fatalism was the legacy of bureaucracy which had also made it difficult for them to take responsibility for anything. I wondered what would allow them to care sufficiently about others. Their hunger for the materialism of the West seemed to be the biggest spur to them to change their lives.

I cheered myself up the following morning 13th April by going shopping and bought the most beautiful sari I had ever seen from the Silk Emporium. I didn't know if I would ever have the courage to put scissors to it or wear it but it was so special I couldn't resist it. It had a gold edging which could only be found in Benares and was subtly iridescent violet and pale green, dependent on how the light caught it. There was something spiritual about it, like sunlight captured in a dewdrop.

Straight after lunch we just managed to catch the tourist bus with four others and we went to see various interesting Buddhist remains. It turned out to be a diverting afternoon. We first looked round a museum where many excavated Buddhist statues had been placed and then went on to the ruins of the old city of Sarnath: considered to be one of the most holy of sites as it was apparently the first place that the Buddha went to after attaining enlightenment at Bodh Gaya.

We learnt that he preached his first discourse here in the deer park and so set in motion what is known as the 'Wheel of the Dharma' and his teachings about how to attain Nirvana and defeat suffering in the endless cycle of birth and rebirth. Sarnath was and continues to be a place of pilgrimage for Buddhists from many countries. Where Buddhism is the major or dominant religion as in Thailand, Japan, Tibet and Ceylon, temples and monasteries were apparently established in the architectural styles of their respective countries. We went into the Japanese Buddhist temple with their beautiful frescoes and very much appreciated being given free tea and oranges.

Our next port of call gave us an extraordinary glimpse into another aspect of the British legacy. We travelled on to the palace of the Maharajah of Benares, which had been partly turned into a museum to show the former grander times of his ancestors. We saw decorated elephants, pictures of Queen Victoria and the various relics and gifts that they had received. We happened to time the visit perfectly. We were outside the palace in the overgrown and unkempt garden listening to the loud, eerie, harsh shrieks of the peacocks as they strutted around, some of them pure white.

Suddenly, all sorts of activity began to take place. Soldiers were mustered, an elderly band gathered together and then the Maharajah stepped out of his palace. The soldiers saluted; the Maharajah saluted. Then the band began to perform the most incredibly amateurish and out of tune rendering of 'Que Sera Sera' while the peacocks continued to shriek and strut. It was so funny that David and I could hardly contain our giggles. The Maharajah stepped into his grand but ancient car, which I visualised would sweep him away proudly to make up for this sad farce, but the car wouldn't start and had to be pushed along by many of the soldiers. It was unreal! All this was very embarrassing to our guide but I couldn't help feeling sorry for the Maharajah. We left the grounds feeling more light-hearted than we had for some time.

The band playing for the Maharajah outside his palace

On Tuesday 14th April David and John got up at 5:15 a.m. to go down to the main ghat to experience that particularly sacred time there. I couldn't face it. Judging by some of the experiences they recounted on their return, it was just as well I hadn't gone as it had been very intense for them. There were huge crowds of people everywhere waiting for the sunrise, going through elaborate rituals before bathing in the Ganges; offering up prayers to the gods, covering themselves in white paint and decking themselves in orange flowers.

They saw many bodies burning, smelt the burning flesh and tried to protect their eyes from the smoke. One sight was so repulsive that David couldn't bring himself to photograph it: it was a body that had been in the water for some time, swollen up like a balloon, pulled out to the middle of the Ganges by a rope. Such is the power of imagination that to this day I feel I was there and that this was my own memory.

Our morning was then ruined by having to wait two hours to reserve a train ticket for Raxaul en-route to Nepal, only to be told that second class tickets could not be reserved! We wandered around aimlessly for much of the afternoon, and I was so exhausted from the heat that had I been given the chance, I would have set off for home. I found that I was getting irritated with David. He seemed to be bossing me around too much and, although as I write this now I feel it was unfair of me, it seemed that I thought he should be protecting me from things that I found difficult. As a result of me trying to talk to David about this, he swore about me to John. I could feel us drifting apart but I tried not to come to any conclusions about it as I realised that we were being severely tested by the extremes of Indian life and weather.

Once on the train that evening, the other passengers started the usual questions to us: 'What is your name please?' 'From which country are you travelling?' 'What is the nature and purpose of your travels?' I noticed that John was now also in a foul mood with the Indians, swearing at them repeatedly. I think part of the problem had occurred when David and John had tried again to get the train reservations in the afternoon and found that the Indians knew how to play that game and had succeeded in pushing David and John out of the way in the process. That was how I felt David was behaving towards me, and when John gave me his sleeping bag on the train, I couldn't help but feel grateful to him.

At the many stops which seemed to be excessively long, people would clamber onto the top of the train and then hang onto the sides, swaying to and fro as it chugged along and rounded the bends on the track.

We dozed fitfully through the night of 15th April. Knowing that Nepal was not too far away now, I found my mood was beginning to get lighter. In fact, a calm seemed to descend on us all. A passenger treated us to snacks and chai, which was very sweet tea where the milk had been added to the tea at the beginning and boiled continually. Another who also seemed friendly invited us to his home though it was unlikely that we could take up the offer. This made me wonder how much the heat was responsible for the way people behaved to each other. We arrived at Muzzaffarpur, one of many gateways to Nepal, three hours late. We learnt that this town had had a disastrous earthquake in 1934 with the loss of many people.

We changed trains and by the time we reached Sagauli, we could see that the scenery was becoming sub-tropical. The villages had mud huts and thatched roofs and were surrounded by banana trees and tall palms. Oxen turned round and round in their circles, grinding corn. Children bathed in the river. The harvesting season was in full swing and outside the sugar cane factory there were about a hundred parked oxen-carts.

At Raxaul, we hoped to sleep in the station while we waited for our train. However, we just couldn't get comfortable on the hard seats so found a bed in a dingy hotel in the town. There was little respite here however: the toilets smelt appalling and there was no water in the shower. The light could not be turned off, the mosquito nets had huge holes in them and we were bitten alive. There was the added anxiety that the mosquitoes carried malaria, a dangerous disease which we had not been protected against. I woke from the little sleep we'd had feeling really sick.

On 16th April we were so glad to be leaving India even though it was only 4:45 in the morning. India was exasperating: so much beauty and so much ugliness. Its people exasperated and exasperating as well: so many of them wanting to leave and to have the life they imagined we had in the west.

Travelling through these different countries, I could see that each had an essential character, even given the individuality of each person and knowing that we had only met a selection of them. I had sensed it every time we crossed a border. I suppose it was a complex interweaving of its inhabitants' beliefs and trust or lack of it, its religion, culture and level of education. It was also what constituted their prime motivations and where they were putting their energy, together with the country's geography and its weather. At the time, India seemed the most complex country I had ever been in.

The journey by bus from Raxaul to Kathmandu was breathtaking and I noticed that my sickness had cleared. Everywhere was so lush and green with many different kinds of trees. For some time, we travelled through a sub-tropical forest beside a river. We were struck by the smiling faces of the Nepalese people everywhere. We noticed that their houses, even in the countryside, were double-storied, often built with bricks or stones and that the roofs were sometimes thatched and sometimes tiled.

The lower foothills were the most beautiful and varied, but as we climbed, the views into the valleys below were wonderful with all the different types of vegetation and always lit up by the jewelled colours of the rhododendrons. We hadn't travelled far before we came across a gigantic python that the locals had killed at the side of the road and the bus stopped so we could all get an opportunity to gaze at this wonder of nature. It was at least ten feet long, (about three metres) and a frightening sight out in the open to our eyes that had only ever seen such creatures safely contained in a zoo.

As we continued our journey, winding our way round one hair pin bend after another skyward, we saw how the Nepalese had created terraces in order to farm every bit of land. The driver brought the bus to a stop again later when he found his way blocked by a huge, overturned lorry. It was the only road to Kathmandu. About a hundred men had gathered round it and all of them working together straining every muscle managed eventually to turn it upright. We caught sight of huge monitor lizards, nearly six feet long; (about 175cm). We also passed an elephant being used to transport logs.

The journey took twelve hours but it was certainly worth every moment. We had climbed to about 8,000 feet and had hoped to get a good view of Everest but it was too cloudy. As we descended again to 4,000 feet into the Kathmandu valley, it became cooler. It was six p.m. when we eventually arrived in Kathmandu and we were very tired. We set off to find a hotel immediately. The local people were beautiful to look at. Tibetans mingled with the Nepalese, and my first impression of the women we met on our walk was that they seemed to have a kind of independence and freedom, working in the cafe and making jokes.

We searched on foot for some time for a decent hotel and eventually found a relatively good one for Kathmandu called The Oriental, which was clean and at least had cold water showers and a courtyard full of bicycles for hire. The beds were as hard as everywhere else here as we had to sleep on wood. We looked around and were taken aback to find Jean already here with the

Spanish couple, Dolores and Martin. He had only $10 left and seemed even crazier than before.

We went looking for something to eat and were surprised by the number of travellers, especially American. We discovered that their existence here had influenced the food on offer and laughed when we found a cafe with toasted peanut butter sandwiches.

It was 17th April and now that we'd arrived at our destination we felt we should be able to relax but we found it hard. We were run-down and worn out. We had also lost a lot of weight. We alternated between sitting around and wandering around, feeling lost without the relentless need to keep travelling onwards. We thought Kathmandu was an incredible place though.

Signs of religion were everywhere, both Hindu and Buddhist: pagodas and temples, small shrines and religious artefacts and grotesque masks that looked as though they were there to scare off evil, carved animals and prayer wheels which people spun as they went past on their daily business. I was reminded of an eastern version of Elizabethan England with its small-scale wooden buildings, ornately carved wooden verandas, very low doors and narrow, dirty streets bustling with people, and pigs, cows and hens roaming around freely. David put it well: he said that the town was like a farm yard with temples instead of pigsties, and stupas instead of cowsheds. The stupas were domed temples which had the Buddha's watchful eyes and eyebrows painted on them on all sides and something resembling a nose but which was the Nepali symbol of unity.

Typical Kathmandu street scene

Group of Nepalese men lounging on a shop front

Resting after the long journey to market

Kathmandu street shrine

Kathmandu street shrine

A wired up temple

Shop keepers lounged around in their allotted spaces all along the road, their scales beside them surrounded by strange local goods and edibles. We were taken by surprise when one shop keeper took out a telephone! It seemed strangely out of place.

Unlike the inhabitants of the other countries we'd travelled through, they did not stare at us; they had become used to travellers of the hippie variety with Kathmandu being the great drug route destination. There were indeed many hippies here, most of them wandering around aimlessly or sitting in the cafes completely stoned. Some had taken on the orange robes and shaven heads of the Buddhist monks. They even had the same blank, inscrutable expression. We noticed that there were a lot of Chinese goods and literature for sale here and some Japanese items.

The road was full of people, many of them carrying huge loads by means of a strap across their foreheads to hold the basket on their backs. Most of them had come down from the hills with their farm produce to sell it in the town and even the children were weighed down. We were horrified to see them wash their beautiful vegetables before selling them in the running streams at the sides of the road where animals and people alike did their business. I understood why they did it because the vegetables looked so shiny and clean afterwards, but the people clearly had no idea about hygiene. Travellers told us that most westerners got ill here and it was not surprising.

The local women decorated both their ears and their noses with a lot of jewellery and wore flowers in their hair. The babies were half-naked. Families sat in the middle of the street picking out nits from each other's hair. There were a few beggars. The butchers shops were quite sinister: the meat was painted in a bright red colour and rows of goats' heads leered at us.

During one of our discussions about our future, David suggested that as we were half way to Australia we should consider going on there, postponing his course place in England and working in Australia for a year. In the end, we decided that we would rather go back to England and I felt relieved. I suspect that I persuaded him that it would be exciting enough to move to Oxford and for him to take up the course in architecture.

We began to have the strange experience of feeling at home and yet not. There were so many restaurants and cafes here that catered for the western palate. They sold lemon tea, beer, French toast, pancakes, peanut and jam sandwiches along with buffalo sandwiches and other local food. It was such a relief from India. And all the time, they played groovy western music such as the Beetles, Traffic, and The Stones. Everyone smoked pot openly. One day, we were amused when a notice came round to say that it was only legal for us to smoke the government sponsored marijuana. One restaurant sold hashish cookies, candy and marijuana pudding!

It was in this restaurant that I began one of the strangest and frightening experiences of my life. As I said before, I was not accustomed to smoke marijuana, finding it neither sociable nor enjoyable as a past-time. However, David, John and Jean thought that it was about time for me to have an experience of being a little stoned and suggested I try the pudding. Once in Ibiza I'd had hashish cookies and they had had very little effect on me so I wasn't feeling overly nervous.

I ate the pudding, which was just a ghastly, gooey, brown mess, and then four Americans came in, sitting at the table next to us and discussed what they would have. When I heard one of them say that one pudding was enough for four people I began to feel apprehensive. However, nothing was happening and John said I would be okay as I'd eaten it with so much sugar. Indeed, I just felt relaxed and was enjoying listening to the Beetles and Cream.

Two hours later, still in the restaurant, I suddenly began to feel stoned and within five to ten minutes, I had really freaked out. First, I felt dizzy and thought I was going to faint so I rested my head on the table. John and David gave me large spoonfuls of sugar which was thought to counteract the effects of marijuana and I ate a jam pancake. But all the time, my mind was going haywire, and I thought I was going to die. I'd never heard of this happening with marijuana but obviously, I'd had a huge overdose. I don't remember much else while I remained in the restaurant except my fear, though I was aware of repetitive things happening in my vision which had become a small, black square. Sometimes these were abstract patterns, sometimes a face and they were all in colour.

As I went out of the restaurant, I remember that I could only see what was in my immediate vision which was now just a narrow tunnel as the usual span of my sight had closed down. It was helpful to have other things to focus on now that we were walking back to the hotel. Then once in our room, although I was still extremely scared, I realised that I was having a very interesting experience, and made a definite decision to notice what was happening. David left me for a time and I sat on the bed, trying to keep conscious; I felt that if I didn't, I would either die or go mad. I tried to keep my eyes open and concentrate on what was closest to my strange vision, which was my body. I looked at my toe and repeated aloud to myself the word 'toe', then 'nail' but found I couldn't keep this up.

All the time, the deepest part of my sub-consciousness was forcing me to leave consciousness, and I had to fight like mad not to lose it. I lay down and felt that I was my whole mind and body, trying to keep all the different parts of myself together. I was sometimes aware of ideas which took physical shape and sometimes aware of feelings which were in specific parts of my body. These caused me much physical discomfort.

There was a pain in the top of my head and also a draining sensation there. I experienced a sort of dizziness in my feet and a tingling in a finger. The top of my mouth felt as if it was curling up. An icy coldness spread from my head down through my body with pain in my ears and excessive dryness in my throat and mouth. I felt I was going to stop breathing at times and then I would hold my head up, breathe deeply and swallow.

Parts of my body floated off and my consciousness tried to pull them back. At one point, part of my brain developed into a protoplasmic-like bulge which made me think of those drawings of heads with strange bulges and 'The Scream' by the Expressionist painter Edvard Munch. Well-known drug use expressions came into my mind as I was literally experiencing the very states they alluded to: 'freaked out', 'flipped my lid' and 'blew my mind'.

I was nearly always conscious of my thoughts becoming concrete, visible and coloured, with different thoughts taking different shapes and colours from various parts of my brain. The darker thoughts came from the deeper recesses of my brain and the darkest thoughts would bring an imperative to consciousness: 'must come to' or 'hold on', and these in turn brought actual symbols to express the demand. For instance, the idea that I must hold on when parts of my body were trying to go into space developed into a boomerang so that these parts would return to me but they were multiplying and growing bigger till they filled my whole mind and I couldn't manage to keep track of them all. It was as though my mind expanded to be my body as well so my foot could actually feel how it was going off from the rest of my body.

Some ideas came as images in straight line blocks, all moving but there was always something deep in the heart of me that wanted me to remain conscious. I tried to open my eyes and to keep them open. The only things that I could concentrate on were things that were close to me and all the time I was in a conflict in this with my consciousness pulling me back deeper inside so couldn't keep my eyes open. Then I thought that if I could only concentrate on something physical about my body with my eyes shut, any idea I could grasp at all or any sensation in my body, it would keep me from losing myself completely.

The struggle was frightening. I was certain at the time that I could lose my mind if I wanted to, but was too frightened to let go. When once I concentrated on my heart, it became so painful, I had to stop. At least I could stop.

What I was aware of was that there was a voice in me making comments about what was happening, and sometimes I told David but he didn't seem interested. He was probably drained by the relentlessness of this too. This voice seemed a sane part of me which I thought of as the watcher who commented, but it was exhausting. Thinking about this a bit later, this watcher reminded me of my university studies into the question of existence in philosophy. We had concluded for example that Déscarte's famous maxim 'Je pense, donc je suis' ('I think, therefore I am') was incorrect as all that could be concluded from an examination of this was that there is thought; not that I exist.

There were distortions in time. For instance, David might say a short sentence and it would seem to take ages to reach me, and it was only after it had reached me that I realised that such a short statement could not have taken long. Once or twice, his voice became distorted and low like a record where the speed has been slowed down. Sometimes, his voice was stretched out like elastic at the end of a sentence, and I had to draw the elastic back so I could find out what the last words were to make sense of what he was saying. While this was happening, there was also the noise of the beetle in the ceiling eating wood, but the sound was exaggerated many times.

I imagined that this episode was more like an acid trip, which I would never have risked, but it was clearly a cannabis overdose trip. It was frightening enough to put me off all drugs for ever.

By the following day Saturday 18th April I was still stoned but had control of my mind at last. It had been a shock to my system and I still had a pain in my head, neck, arms and hands, and felt dazed and very tired. The whole thing had lasted for about twenty four hours. However, in the evening, we took a pleasant but exhausting walk up to Swayambhunath complex which everyone referred to as the Monkey Temple because of all the monkeys that lived there and which were thought to be holy. It was a Buddhist temple and the most sacred of all Buddhist sites, beloved also by the Tibetans. Although it was quite a climb from the town, - it is claimed that there are 365 steps to the top of the temple, - the views over the Kathmandu valley were spectacular.

Swayambhunath Stupa

On Sunday 19ᵗʰ April I was relieved to feel back to my normal self and we set about getting information about a trek into the Himalayas and a permit. We were told that we should not take any photos. David also sought some facts about Nepal. The population was 10.5 million in 1961; literacy was 10% of the population; 93% were involved in agriculture; the snowline was 16,000 feet and Kathmandu was 700 miles from the nearest sea.

I found myself wondering about the other young travellers that we were meeting here. There were many draft dodgers holed up in the cafes, glad to be clear of the war in Vietnam. Others seemed discontent with the societies they had left behind and were seeking something different and more satisfying. I guess there was also a natural curiosity about parts of the world other than their own. Those young men who had shaved their heads and wrapped themselves in an orange cloth, trying to lead a Buddhist life had perhaps found what they were looking for, though I don't remember talking to them. Others were entertaining and looking after young urchins and child beggars.

But so many that we met and talked to were primarily interested in drugs, and in particular, in acid and opium. One young man told us he got ill when he took opium and ill if he didn't and he was hallucinating all the time whether he had taken anything or not. He said he was experimenting with drugs partly to see if he could produce better music but had found that the opposite was true.

We noticed how so many of the travellers were stoned all day and every day and we could see that it made dull, everyday things fascinating to them. For instance, two stoned American men had made their orders in the cafe that day. One had asked for drinking chocolate but had been brought tea instead. His friend exclaimed, 'Wow! This is real freaky land!' Though David and I would never understand why they should live this way when life was so interesting and enjoyable without drugs, we could see that so many younger people were turned on to new possibilities and new ways of seeing things with or without drugs that western society would never be the same again.

The following day 20th April was also very relaxing. We went round the markets and David bargained with a seller for a woollen jerkin, and knocked his price down from 25 to 18 rupees. My thoughts were very much with England that day and I was wondering how we would earn money with David due to be studying for the next seven years and with only a small grant. I considered buying some Tibetan belts and bags and perhaps some shirts from Kabul on the way back. I wondered about the possibility of bringing back some semi-precious stones.

The next day 21st April we decided to make preparations for our trek in the Himalayan Mountains to Helambu. Unfortunately though, there was tension amongst us, and by the evening, I was not sure that I wanted to go. John could not decide whether he wanted to go back to Europe or return to Australia, in which case, he would only accompany us for part of the journey. Ultimately, we decided to cancel that trip and find another way of seeing the countryside and the high mountains.

During the day, we met an English guy who had left home two years ago without a penny, looking for a good environment and had never worked since then. He simply begged or found what he needed and his parents were sending him just £2 a month. He had a rather sweet, gentle nature and had now done with dropping acid. He told me that my bad experience was common amongst bad trips and was known as disintegration of the body.

He had had enough travelling and planned to go back in about five month's time. Like us, he was looking forward to being back in England and to the comforts there. He said that most people who had experienced a bad drug trip eventually come out of it, however bad a state they were in. On the other hand, there were two guys in Kathmandu who had taken an acid trip a year ago and still hadn't come through it. To most people, they would seem mad, but he felt they would come back eventually. I wasn't so sure.

We also met an Australian woman who had been travelling for five years, working for six months or so of each year wherever she could find work. Like so many of the Australians we met, she didn't want to go home. She told us that she enjoyed working in psychiatric hospitals best because she felt she could be herself completely and didn't need to put on an act. She also found that most of the patients had a great sense of peace. They were probably medicated up to the eyeballs actually. She loved London but she kept moving because she had a mental map of the world in her mind which had to be followed. She obviously had something in common with David here.

We read in the local paper that Nepalese teachers were not being paid enough. One of the ideas to cope with this was for children in rural schools to grow vegetables and fruit and then to give the proceeds from their sale to the teachers. In the town schools, where carpentry was taught, children could sell their furniture. What an ingenious idea: pragmatic, communal and relevant! Simple ideas often seemed to make more sense and be more effective than when the bureaucrats got involved and the great capitalist machine began its self-serving slow grind.

On Wednesday 22nd April we told John that we'd decided not to go on the trek, and during the course of the day, it was clear that we were all relieved. John decided that he would try and get back to Australia for the wedding. I also talked to David about the two of us apparently growing apart, and he responded in a way that was really helpful. He felt that having John with us since Kabul had put a strain on our relationship and ability to share experiences. Also, he said that there had been so much in India to assimilate that it had taken us rather deeply along different paths as all deep experiences can do. He admitted that he'd grown a shell around himself in reaction to many of these experiences because he couldn't rationalise them and had been left feeling strange and cut-off. I felt relieved by this discussion.

We cycled to Pashupatinath Temple – the holiest of Hindu temples in Nepal, devoted to Shiva, the Lord of all animals. It was said to have been built in 400 AD and was located in the eastern part of Kathmandu on the banks of the Bagmati River. Only born Hindus were allowed to go into the temple so all we could do was admire it from the banks of the river, but it was very beautiful, both in its pagoda-type architecture and in its surrounding countryside. The roofs were embellished with gold and the doors of silver, and it stood by a shallow, wide river, which was crowded with temples and shrines along its banks.

I was happy that there were no crowds when we were there. Although Hindu pilgrims came every day, they only came in great numbers for the special festival days and nights. They also had public cremations, though we never saw any and I was glad that the feeling there was so different from Benares, surrounded as Pashupatinath was with hills, forests and meadows.

Many monkeys had made their home there and we enjoyed watching their antics and relaxed in the atmosphere and beauty of the place. For much of the time though, we were kept company by a group of young, savvy urchins who had learnt to speak English very well and had organised themselves into a group money-making enterprise. They hired themselves out to us as our tour guides while one of them made it his business to watch our bikes for us. They also treated us to a little show, singing a song while a boy of about five years old danced.

Later, as we walked along the river bank, we were aware of a commotion. A young monkey had climbed along an electric cable above us and received a nasty shock. Immediately, a group of monkeys began to surround us with what were clearly cries of aggression, and we had to beat a very hasty retreat. We also saw two water snakes winding their way up river, frightening the locals who had been doing their washing there. On our return journey at a roundabout, we noticed a bull about to mate with a cow right in the middle of the road. The pedestrians had gathered at the sides of the road to watch.

On Thursday 23rd April we spent much of the morning procrastinating because of various difficulties about where to go and ironically, given the tensions, because John wasn't around and we were missing him. Eventually, we set off alone and walked to the foot of the hill of the Monkey Temple where we relaxed and did some writing and reading. We climbed a little higher to eat our lunch of bread, cheese and papaw, and found we were being watched by some vicious looking monkeys. It wasn't long before the first one leapt up at David in an attempt to snatch his cheese, and as we attempted to make a quick getaway, I was followed by another. One managed to grab the packet of cheese but David wasn't going to let the monkey get away with it and succeeded in making it put the cheese down. In the end, we had to give up the idea of eating our picnic on the hill and leave.

It was lovely there, - quite Alpine-looking. I found I was aware of each tree, person and cow in a very special way and could feel my connection to them all. I wondered if that was how it was for someone who was gently stoned. The Nepalese people were so friendly, especially the women, and the Tibetans seemed even more so with their round moon faces and big grins. Their noses and ears were generally covered in heavy-looking silver jewellery, often with gems of turquoise and coral, and it seemed that it was they who had brought so many of the fine handicrafts to Nepal.

On Friday 24th April, having decided on a shorter mountain trek that John had the time to do, we set off for Nagarkot, 32 kilometres east of Kathmandu, in blazing sunshine. We hoped to catch sight of the sun rising over Mount Everest at dawn the following day so we needed to travel fast. We caught an early morning bus to Bhadgaon, which was once the capital of Nepal hundreds of years ago. We didn't have time to stop there but planned to return another time to look at the impressive buildings, carvings and shrines.

We walked from the town through the corn meadows along a narrow sun-baked earthen ledge and then began our ascent along a fairly wide path. The surrounding countryside was amazing with bright sun-lit greens, yellows and really hot oranges of wheat, barley and millet in their rhythmic, parallel rows, often in terraces. Along the way, a child showed us how to get to a pool where we could swim and cool off. En-route, we passed many men and women harvesting their crops: cutting down the wheat and tying it into bunches by swinging it round and round, separating the wheat from the chaff just as the farmers in England had done a hundred and fifty or so years ago.

The hot colours of the corn fields

Farming in the terraced corn fields

The first pool we came to was man-made. As we were saving all the money we could, we declined to pay the 1.50 rupees we were asked for and climbed up the stony river bed where we discovered a beautiful, natural and deep pool which had been created by a waterfall. The place was further enhanced by the trees and shrubs that surrounded it. We were asked for one rupee this time, but though it seems so mean now, we didn't pay it, our rationalisation being because it hadn't been made by anyone. I suppose we had become fixated in our mindset of having to save money at all costs.

David thought it was too dirty to swim in and was concerned about the possibility of snakes and leeches but our young guide assured us that there weren't any so we got in and enjoyed our cooling swim. However, it wasn't totally relaxing in the water as I remembered the two water snakes that had terrified the women doing their washing after our visit to the Pashupatinath Temple.

Refreshed, we began a very steep climb up a rocky hill above the river. Knowing that there were another three miles to go, with my breath getting shorter and my fear of heights, I began to panic. The young boy told us that we needed a guide for 10 rupees each because of the dangerous jungle and many paths that we could get lost on. We had decided before we set off that day that we could manage without a guide. The boy had originally told us that he had only joined us so that he could improve his English so when he asked for money we refused and it became rather unpleasant. However, we eventually continued upwards on our own and as it was so steep, I was relieved to rest in a glade and have the lunch we'd brought.

Then we continued slowly up the hill till we came to a road. I was exhausted and I'm sure David was tired but we continued and I felt I could hardly put one foot in front of the other. Suddenly, we heard a vehicle coming behind us and were pleased to think that we could have a lift, but it failed to stop for us. We were disappointed to discover that it was a group of Swiss tourists and that they had passed us even though they must have seen how tired we were.

I think we were experiencing something of the relativity of poverty and wealth that day, and we would probably never know the wealth of those who travelled in comfort nor what it was to be as poor as the local people. They were uneasy lessons for us. Later, a local truck did stop for us and we were able to rest for about three quarters of a mile until we were dropped at the foot of what we were to discover was the final part of the climb. We didn't know this at the time however and thought later that they were probably not allowed to give us lifts and accept money because they were not official tourist drivers.

After seven or eight miles of climbing, tired and thirsty, we were so relieved to reach our lodge, even though it couldn't have been more basic. A slight drizzle and wind were welcoming. We were soon joined by a young Australian woman, travelling on her own. She told us that she had been camping on the ridge at the edge of the jungle but had been warned by the soldiers that there were leopards about. Since she only had a small blunt knife with her, she had decided to come down to the lodge. I was very impressed by her courage in travelling alone like this. Amazingly, during the introductions, she and John realised that they had colleagues in common back in Australia.

She was very pessimistic about her country. She said they were a self-satisfied people with a rugged image that wasn't really true of them. They were exceedingly pro-America due to their fear of the Communists which is why they had sent in soldiers alongside the Americans in Vietnam. She added that they were anti-intellectual, closed-minded and uninterested in change.

They also had the White Policy, which was the exclusion of all non-European immigrants into Australia for fear of damaging the culture they had built up. She thought that the only interesting things went on in the universities but that most students settled into the rut of conventionality once they'd left. She said that Europe generally was far more interesting and that she planned to take up a place she'd been offered in a London university to read for an M.A. and that she would become a writer.

The following morning Saturday 25ᵗʰ April just before dawn broke, we got up and watched for the sun to rise above Mount Everest. It rose as an orange ball but the hot weather had come in early this year by a week and brought with it early morning mists so we only saw an outline of Mount Everest and the other high mountain ranges. It was rather disappointing but in any case, who would have thought that we would ever have got so close to witnessing this sight! We had climbed without a guide and stood in this fantastic place with no tourists. We'd planned our trip while in Ibiza with absolutely no idea of what it would all entail. No doubt we had made this part of our trip, like so much of the rest of it in too short a time. Officially, it was probably a two day trek with a guide.

We set off down the mountain with the Australian woman in beautiful sunshine with glorious views of the Kathmandu valley. We stopped again at the pool and John and I took several dips. We built a small fire to boil up some tea. We enjoyed this along with some curried chips, some biscuits and a slice of bread and cheese. Once we'd resumed our journey down, practically every child we passed asked us for money or cigarettes, and one four year old shocked us when he asked for cannabis. We also had a welcome bowl of curds and whey. Whey was somewhat like tough Rice Crispies. It had no flavour but it added bulk and crunch to the curds.

We arrived back by six p.m. and although still tired and over-heated, the return journey had been a lot easier than we'd anticipated. We fell into our beds as soon as we got back to the hotel. There was another mini monsoon during the night with lashings of rain and much thunder and lightning and by morning it looked just as thundery.

We spent Sunday 26th April relaxing in our rooms, reading and writing and I reflected a little on Nepal. It was so beautiful with amazingly varied scenery: semi-tropical in the south, oriental and alpine in the foothills and the highest mountain range in the world with their bleak, frozen peaks. The people smiled a lot, apparently contented and playful. Likewise, I had never seen an angry or miserable Tibetan face even though they were forced to flee to Nepal when the Chinese invaded their country twenty years earlier. How interesting that one set of people would be able to smile after such an event while others in different parts of the world would seek retribution.

It was true that the Tibetans were surrounded by great natural beauty and the Nepalese did not seem to mind them living amongst them. They had allowed Buddhism and Hinduism to exist side by side in a very natural way; but I wondered if there was more to it to cause such a different reaction: perhaps something in the Buddhist religion which taught both acceptance of change as well as personal responsibility and showed in practical ways how to become more enlightened. The national character must have been influenced by the religion anyway. Of course, there was no possibility of Tibet fighting such a powerful country as China, but the Tibetans could have become morose, defeated or angry and they hadn't. They were an amazing example to others.

I could see that Nepal and Tibet were at the geographical centre of Asia, so for acquisitive countries seeking power, they were vulnerable. I had no idea if they also contained valuable resources. I was aware of the proliferation of Chinese propaganda here, and indeed, we had acquired a copy of Chairman Mao's 'Little Red Book'.

We wondered if the monsoon rains had arrived early along with the unusually hot summer. The mists had set in and the dark, heavy thunder clouds settled over Kathmandu, occasionally lit up with lightning. We considered leaving and taking longer on the journey back. John had decided to leave for home in a couple of days and I felt some relief about this as there was huge tension between him and David now. John seemed to need mothering and a lot of loving and this seemed to bring out aggression in David. John admitted himself that his mother was the only reason he had decided to go back to Australia. Thinking about this now, we all felt something of what John was able to feel openly.

On Monday 27th April we enjoyed watching part of the wedding celebrations of a wealthy family. Two bands came and stood on the street outside the house and took it in turns to play. One of them was quite polished and accomplished but the other was more interesting as it gave the impression that each member of the band was free to improvise: the result was an exciting blend of musical styles.

The two wedding cars were highly decorated with paper flowers, and then four men came and stood at the four corners of the cars with large, lit candles. I wondered if they were to ward off evil spirits. Then the bride's mother, covered from the neck down in exquisitely embroidered cloth, was carried round the first car then put inside it. The bride, similarly enveloped in a beautiful cloth, was then helped round the second car by some women. All these women were wailing loudly, which was intriguing. Then there followed a small procession of relatives together with the bridegroom who had a garland of flowers on his head. They all stepped into the car and were driven off.

More monsoon-like rain started at 6 p.m. but we were told that it was pre-monsoon rain. I felt both relief and sadness at the thought of John's departure the following day. We had shared so much with him in England and Ibiza and then in four of the other countries of our journey.

On Tuesday 28ᵗʰ April John left for Calcutta on his way back home to Australia. I wondered how this would change David's and my experience. We had been so fond of him in England and Ibiza but the hardships and unknowns of the sort of travels that we had been on since then had put a strain on our relationships and I hoped that his departure would improve mine with David.

It was a beautiful sunny day and we set off for the swimming pool in the Palace Gardens. They kept the gardens well with roses and pansies, shrubs and trees. There were also lots of pools with huge fish, and one had a large reclining statue of a god, painted in parts in red and yellow and in front of which some people had come to worship. The swimming pool itself was wonderful with only a few others in it: mainly playful, happy Sherpas. It seemed to be Olympic in size, was clean and boarded on one side with flowers and on the other with grass and trees leading up to a wooded hill. We got quite sunburnt there for the first time.

In the evening, we went to the 'Tibetan Dragon' restaurant and had an interesting conversation with three L.S.D. / Acid enthusiasts from different parts of the world. In fact, only two really talked as the third said that he found discussion disturbed his peace of mind. The Australian told us in a rambling way that he had hallucinated at the 'Monkey Temple' and thought he was Shiva and that a Hindu visitor had actually taken him for Shiva! I could see some sort of connection between Acid and Shiva since both were about destruction. These men said they had never been aware of vibrations until they took Acid, and their own vibrations seemed pretty mellow, though there was a sort of evangelical tone in the way they spoke about Acid.

The American, who was twenty five years old, had started smoking cannabis at the age of eleven and had been on Acid for nearly as long. He said that he had taken four hundred and seventy five trips. In the last ten years his trips had become religious. He reckoned that the ones with Acid had made him care about others and stopped him using others to satisfy his own needs. Previously, he hadn't even credited others with intelligence. He also admitted to having taken on many bad roles in life, including being a drug dealer, a prostitute pimp and a criminal. I must say, it was hard to imagine this as he had the face of an angel.

He said that two of his hallucinations were important to him: one was that he was the god, Ganesha: the elephant headed son of Shiva and Parvati. The other hallucination had given him proof of God and had taken place quite recently. While tripping, he had lost a cuff link on a beach in Goa and had searched all over for it. He paused from his searching, and saw a shaft of light come down and land on a spot on the sand. He went over to it but could see nothing, so he put his hand down about three inches into the sand and lo and behold, there was the cuff link. This was not the first time that I'd heard 'trippers' talking about God in terms of light. He went on to tell us of many other occasions when things had seemed impossible but where chanting had solved the problems. For instance, they had given their last 60 pais to a beggar in India and then received 10 rupees from some Westerners.

He also told us that he'd met a woman whom he referred to as his female twin who was using the 'I Ching'. He had not encountered this ancient Chinese book of divination before. David and I had enjoyed using it back in England as it contained much ancient wisdom based on the synchronicity of one's question with the answering hexagram. It was very popular with those interested in alternative culture at the time. He had expressed interest in the book.

Apparently, this woman was planning to go to Europe and he to Kathmandu. Later, however, she had turned up in Kathmandu and presented him with the 'I Ching' which he'd begun to base his life on. Then last night, she had returned and told him that she wanted it back and he had realised that the time had come to put into practice all that he had learnt without continuing to rely on the 'I Ching'. He said he would make progress in this way and then perhaps the book would come his way again and he'd learn some more.

This American impressed me in how he had turned around his life. Somehow he had been able to leave behind using others for his needs and making a living out of them. He had now become a warm, accepting person, interested in the deeper things of life and wanting to learn and grow. I felt he'd given joy to many others along the way too, but the concern still remained for me that these people relied on L.S.D. to keep them like this. How would they fare without it? He had admitted that he realised it was a dangerous drug and that he felt nervous before every trip. He had many friends who had gone mad and were in mental asylums, and one man who had never again been able to utter a word. Apart from him saying, 'And we dropped Acid on the full-moon,' he left me feeling in a good space and he told me he felt better too for talking to us.

I was beginning to wonder how all my experiences would affect my teaching, though I still had a strong desire to teach.

On Wednesday 29th April we cycled to Patan, famous for its arts and crafts, and made several purchases. David bought an apparently rare Tibetan coin which cost 40 rupees (about thirty three old shillings), a Tibetan brass seal for 35 rupees, three old Nepalese coins from a girl for 1.20 rupees and a lion statue for his mother. It was so hot, and when we sat in Durbar Square to rest, we were continually pestered by children. We looked around some of the shrines and temples which apparently had finer carvings than those in Kathmandu but I'm afraid we had become tired of looking round so many.

We sat on the grass outside one temple near some Tibetans who were also on the grass. The women and children were so colourful with flowers in their hair and they formed half a square while the men sat in a line behind them. Then several of the men took different foods round to the women and children, putting a portion of each on a large, round leaf. Some of the women followed, pouring out water to drink. It was a colourful scene, and David wanted to take some photos. However, some of the women weren't too happy about this, so we decided to move away, but first, they gave us a taste of some of their food: one was some incredibly hot spice and the other, some small, hard, black beans which were quite tasty. A little later, we were amused to see them holding black umbrellas over themselves as sunshades.

Back in a cafe in Kathmandu, listening yet again to Acid freaks, I found myself getting bored with them. One woman told us that she dropped Acid or used hard drugs every day and seemed proud of the fact that she often ended up in hospital. Another woman who'd been in Kathmandu for months and looked thin and unwell was obviously lonely and lost. One guy tried to explain the wonders of his trip but he was virtually inarticulate.

Another woman tried to articulate it this way: 'I just dig the vibrations of Kathmandu. It's a really groovy place for trips.'

Her companion replied, 'I had a really difficult trip last night. It just blew my mind. I dropped Acid in the light of the moon at The Bakery and I just couldn't tear myself away. I went back in time and everything, and it was like there were two halves in my mind - good and evil.'

Woman: 'Yes, you really feel those vibrations.'

Man: 'Then this cat came towards me and he was like he was in anguish, and I kind of felt it come in me. And like, man, that's difficult 'cause normally I just feel me.'

Woman: 'That's really groovy. I had something similar.'

The man didn't have anything to add to this. Acid as well as cannabis, seemed to take people into themselves in new ways from their previous experience but perhaps it was something else already in a person that brought about either positive or negative change in them later. Another guy was just staring wildly into space while neurotically and rhythmically stroking his companion's hair, and making weird noises to the music. I wasn't at all keen on any of their vibrations and if I didn't judge them intellectually, I certainly recoiled from them emotionally.

On Thursday morning 30th April we went to Bhatgaon by bus eight miles away but unfortunately I found it too hot and didn't have the energy or desire to look at anything really. It was a good example of a Nepalese Pagoda type temple with three to five tiers and it seems that we missed the erotic carvings there through our heat-induced apathy and ignorance of their existence. I enjoyed the screen and paper paintings in the art gallery though where both Buddhist and Hindu painters had really let their imaginations run wild with gods and monsters in beautiful colours.

We got back in time for a late lunch and then spent quite a lot of time in 'The Tea Room' hoping to meet two guys who'd advertised for two passengers to travel with them in their car to Benares. They never turned up.

It was now Friday 1st May. We learnt that the two guys with the lift on offer had changed their minds and were now going to Calcutta, so we did our shopping, then walked three miles in the heat to see one of the processions to celebrate the marriage of the Prince and Princess of Nepal. We waited three hours for a procession that lasted about twenty minutes and which was mainly composed of soldiers and bands.

Some of the local bands were interesting with what we presumed were dancers but they didn't do any dancing during the procession. They were dressed in tribal gear, sometimes with masks, and some of the men were dressed in hairy animal skins. There were also some giant figures, really grotesque, representing the different jobs of the people. The procession started with some soldiers marching and firing shots into the air continuously, perhaps to shoot away evil spirits. We had some concern for a watcher who had positioned himself in a tree for a good view of the proceedings!

The princess, who looked very beautiful, rode in an open carriage with her two maids, and the prince came later on the canopied seat of an enormous and wonderfully decorated elephant. At this sight, the crowds broke into spontaneous clapping.

Later, we met a German guy who told us that Ceylon was the most beautiful country he'd ever seen, with inexpensive and clean places to stay, lots to do and pleasant, simple people. We hadn't thought of going on to Ceylon but he had caught our interest. In the evening, we went back to the hotel and worked out our finances and time schedule as best we could in the circumstances. It seemed incredible, but we discovered that we probably had exactly the right amount of money left, and as far as we could judge it, the right amount of time if we left Kathmandu pretty soon. It would give us two weeks in Ceylon and would entail two rather long journeys through India and a very hot time of it. We would also have to go through Calcutta so we wondered if the two men were still looking for passengers.

We spent the following morning 2nd May with Carla and Marco, who confirmed for us that we should visit Ceylon in spite of the heat and the long journeys through India. It had also become very hot in Kathmandu.

Sunday 3rd May was our last day there, and we had a lot to do to prepare for our journey. We sold quite a few of our items of clothing and after our meals for the day we had three rupees left over for the next day's food. By the end of the day we were pretty tired but excited at the prospect of seeing Ceylon.

As usual, there were many 'Acid freaks' in 'The Tea Room' with their usual clichés:

Man: 'Took a trip and it was terrible, man; just like I was wallowing in my own shit.' Woman: 'Yeah, I just dig that scene. We gave Alan his first trip and it was just beautiful...... When Ann left, she was so beautiful....... Were there many beautiful people in Calcutta?'

And so on, ad nauseam. It was definitely time to leave.

On Monday 4th May, after eighteen days in Kathmandu, we took a bus to Raxaul, and the bus seemed to promise more comfort than usual until we started our journey. We were continually thrown from side to side with all the bends in the road. The further we travelled the hotter it became which somehow detracted from the beauty of the scenery.

I tried to sum up my feelings about what we'd experienced in Nepal, though I hadn't written much in my journal for five days. Staying there had certainly given us an opportunity to rest after our fast, uncomfortable and exhausting journey through extremes of weather across the Middle East and Asia. We had met many drug-loving travellers there who seemed hung up on tripping. Had they come all this way simply to be able to take drugs every day or were they genuinely interested in the countries and the people they were visiting? How many of them would grow as people and change for the better for that experience? How were they and us affecting the people whose countries we were staying in?

We had seen some incredibly varied and beautiful countryside and a way of life that had hardly changed over hundreds of years. We had witnessed the happy assimilation of Tibetans into Nepal and Buddhism alongside Hinduism and their integration into everyday life. We had learnt that the illiteracy rate was about 95% and that the average life expectancy was only 32 years.

We certainly felt that the Nepalese were much happier than the Indians we'd met so far but of course we weren't able to talk with them. Some travellers had told us that they were mean and that the shop keepers ignored them. We ourselves hadn't encountered that behaviour at all however. We had also been told by one traveller that the Tibetans were unfriendly to people trekking in the mountains or ignored them, but of course we didn't know what had really gone on in those situations and it was quite possibly a misunderstanding between different cultures.

We weren't searched at Raxaul station but we had a scary experience. We had met up with Marco and Carla again and were sitting on the platform watching amazingly bright glows all over the sky from electric storms when a sudden and cold wind rose up and within a minute it was gale force. Before we even had time to consult each other or do anything, we were in the middle of a dust storm, scarcely able to breathe and could see nothing in front of us. We'd heard of whirlwinds killing people in Calcutta that year and we didn't know how dangerous this would be. It felt as though we would be suffocated and I wondered if we would get through it.

I don't know how long it lasted as we were just intent on staying alive in the moment but eventually it began to rain and gradually the dust began to settle. We looked at each other and saw that we were ingrained everywhere from head to foot in a thick, black coating. We laughed at the sight of each other and as much as anything from relief. There was nothing to be done now but to wait for the train. The Spanish couple headed for Patna and promised to leave a note for us at Poste Restante when they reached Teheran. We told them we would send them word from Colombo or wherever we were once we knew our plans.

Eventually, our train arrived, and we got in, blacker than coal sweeps. We were quick enough to get seats, thank God, as we had a twenty six hour journey ahead of us to Calcutta with three train changes.

On our final train journey, we met two interesting men who seemed sincere. They told us a few things about the Indian government. They said that the government members were corrupt and cited the example of asking for money from people to help some cause, only to pocket it themselves. They said that there was no unity in the government since there were about sixty political parties. I also wondered how they found the money for a space programme when there was so much needing to be done at home.

We discussed the question of race and immigration too and we told them that there were good things to come out of the arrival of other races in the West, now beginning in parts of England; that it could make us more understanding and tolerant of other cultures, religions and ways. I said that there was always a fear of 'otherness' in people, both individually and nationally, whether in the colour of skin or in the challenges that came when we thought that only our way of doing things was the right way.

It was true that when foreigners from one country settled in another in specific places, it could lead to mistrust, possessiveness and a feeling that the country was being 'taken over'. We also had to face the fact that Britain had done its share of imposing itself on other countries, as India and Pakistan knew only too well. In the long run, however, even though it brought tensions, the arrival of other races in England would, I felt, enrich us. One of the men was so interested in this conversation that he forgot to get out at his station!

It was now 5th May and we eventually arrived in Calcutta. Our first impressions of this city were not favourable. We were cheated by the taxi driver then offered a disgusting room for 20 rupees. There was an enormous rat there and the room was crawling with two inch long cockroaches! Luckily though, we found another hotel: Model Lodge, which was cheap and comfortable enough and which suited us fine.

The following day 6ᵗʰ May was very colourful. We were cheated often but found ourselves growing tolerant of it, and the truth was that we also experienced a lot of kindness here. We started off with brunch in a Hong Kong restaurant and then went about the tricky business of getting concessions for our next train journey. We took a rickshaw to the ticket office, pulled by a running man. These, along with the ones pulled by cyclists, made me feel uneasy: the men were always so skinny and they strained every muscle to take us on our journey. Besides which, it was so hot and humid. We noticed some beautifully kept tropical gardens en-route.

By now, we knew roughly what the cost of a ride should be and at the end of it, he asked us for an extortionate amount which we were unwilling to pay. Crowds soon gathered around us as they had in Delhi, but unlike what happened there, these crowds took an objective stance, really wanting to sort it out for both parties. One man, who seemed more educated than the others, decided on a price for us. It was more expensive than if we had taken a taxi, but we were happy to accept it.

Against all expectations, we had no trouble at all getting concessions, and went later to New Market to look at ankle bracelets. Unfortunately, we weren't at all sure that what we were being shown was silver and they were each asking 65 rupees for the heavy ones. We enjoyed several drinks there including a coconut one and one with sugar cane and limes.

We were pestered non-stop by men whose job it was presumably to get customers to the shops and thereby gain commission. This behaviour wasn't conducive to our spending any money and had us walking all over the place comparing prices and finding that what we discovered ourselves did indeed cost less. We did purchase some things and discovered later when looking at similar things at the station that we had paid far more in the market. I guess they were used to wealthy tourists at the market and we were fair game.

Before I'd arrived in Calcutta I must admit that I'd been anxious about going there because of the terrible things we'd heard about it. It was true that it was very dirty and as soon as we had arrived at the station, we had seen so many homeless, malnourished people just lying on the ground outside that we'd had to step carefully over them. We were told that about a quarter of a million people slept out on the streets. We also knew that those that died in the night were picked up and put into 'death carts' in the morning. We were conscious also of stepping around very ill people including those with leprosy whose bodies were disintegrating. It was so difficult to come to terms with all this suffering and to face it at every moment. I had no idea what the most healing response could be. It was overwhelming.

However, in spite of the dirt and the huge numbers of people, there were some beautiful flowering trees there and plenty of fruit to eat and coconuts to drink on every street corner. Our impressions of Calcutta by the time we left were very favourable compared with those of Delhi. We wondered how much of this was due to our being without the company of John and Jean who had drawn trouble to themselves and us by their involvement with drugs. Everything had certainly become much easier since we'd gone our separate ways and people were much kinder to us and seemed genuinely interested as opposed to being superficially curious.

It was now Thursday 7th May and we faced a thirty six and a half hour journey third class! Unfortunately, we had been unable to book sleepers on the train to Madras (now known as Chennai) but at least we had managed to get reserved seats. This time, there was a guard present checking that only those with tickets actually got on the train, so for the first time we had some space and felt optimistic about the journey to come.

However, such feelings were short-lived. Three stops later in quick succession, the guard didn't stand a chance of doing his job and the dirty carriage became packed out. Soon there were five people to every three space seat! There were people on top of the train and hanging out of the doors and the windows. The noise increased as did the heat. Eventually it rose to about 103 degrees Fahrenheit (about 40 degrees Celsius.) The train could only move sluggishly. Baggage was piled high and people were also sitting all over the floor of the carriage and corridor as well as in the luggage racks.

A passing crowded train

To get to the toilet, we actually had to step on top of people because they were sprawled all along the floor with no space between them! It was inhuman to step on people like this. When we eventually got to the tiny cabin at the end of the corridor, the toilet itself was simply a hole in the floor. Then we had to face repeating the shameful assault to those people on the floor on our return back to our spot.

Sleep was out of the question, though I found a period of rest when a man offered me his place on the luggage rack! I was glad that I was young, fit and healthy. To be old in this situation didn't bare thinking about.

People continued to be friendly to us and to each other and we wondered if people from the east and south of India were simply a happier people than in the north. In any case, I found myself far more tolerant of and compassionate towards these people even when they were being emotionally or materially demanding, because, unlike the ones we had met in Delhi, they suffered from very real hardship. I really got that they needed to fight for their survival. We too in our own ways were experiencing the feelings of resignation that grow out of hardship and the powerlessness to do anything about it.

I also noticed that even those Indians who like ourselves had reserved seats were completely accepting of those who came and took up their space without a ticket, even though it meant that they would suffer. No doubt, years of being resigned to living with the way it was contributed to that, but there was also graciousness about this acceptance, and if Hinduism was the reason for this, well then, it was a kind and pragmatic religion.

The countryside was full of palm trees and the leaves from these had been used to make the roofs of the village huts. Every so often at the station stops, food sellers would lean in through the window and ask if there was anything we wanted to drink or eat. Some kind of cola was always on offer but we usually drank their chai. We bought various spicy finger snacks which we'd never had before, and were very happy with that.

We arrived at Central Station in Madras early in the morning of Friday 8th May after another more or less sleepless night. We were exhausted, sticky and green-black dirty from the smoke of the steam engine. Our bums were sore. We felt almost delirious with happiness when we found a good station restaurant and had a somewhat English breakfast of fried eggs and chips, followed by bread and jam and washed down with lemon tea.

We didn't have to go far from the station before we found the clean and inexpensive hotel that we'd been recommended called Everest Lodge. I took a much needed shower and went straight to bed, while David, who suddenly felt energetic, went off in heat of 102.2 degrees Fahrenheit to get train tickets and concessions to Rameshwaram. He returned three hours later with tickets, tired after being sent back and forth between Central and Egmore Stations quite needlessly, but with a sense of achievement. David enjoyed a situation that tested his metal.

View of slum dwellers from our hotel balcony in Madras

Bullock cart in Madras

Hand carts in Madras

We stayed in the hotel for our dinner in the evening and loved our Thali meal - a typical Indian meal with its selection of small dishes. After that, we walked around Madras for a while. We noticed that the Indians here had much darker skins, almost black. On our return to the hotel, some urchins caught hold of us and dragged us into a shop where materials were sold, asking for some material. Although we felt really sorry for the dirty, ragged state they were in, we knew that had we complied with their request, numerous other children would have begged us to clothe them. Apart from that, we needed our money to make sure we could get home.

On Saturday 9th May we had an interesting day, though we were not successful in getting concessions for our journey to Rameswarum as the office was closed. More than anywhere else, we saw terribly ill people. Some were just lying in the middle of the street with diseases that I couldn't even bear to describe and everybody just walking past. One man had a horrible growth coming out of his stomach and his family were just sitting all around him as he lay on the pavement while his children begged for food. It was heart-breaking and I couldn't understand how the government could allow such suffering when they were so comfortable and were seeking international recognition for achievements in their space programme. How could people face such things daily and feel okay about their own comfortable lives?

We took a bus out to the sandy beach of Marina-Madras and heard that while we had been on that interminable train journey the temperature had risen to 109 degrees Fahrenheit (42 degrees Celsius), much hotter than usual. Even the Indians were finding it unbearable. It was wonderful to arrive at the beach with its cooler temperature of 96 degrees Fahrenheit. We felt the joy of sea water on our feet for the first time since we'd left Ibiza. But even in the shallows I was aware of just how dangerous that sea was. It had a nearly vertical drop down into deep water and my feet were constantly pulled towards it by the enormous power of the current from the Bay of Bengal as the waves returned to the ocean.

Finding some pretty shells compensated somewhat for the fact that our feet were being roasted on the hot sand. We watched the fishermen attempting to take out their primitive sailing boats that had been formed from loose-fitting logs, fighting with the huge breakers and being beaten back to shore over and over again. Any catches they managed to make were of small, silver fish.

After a while, we walked along the front and took a bus into the countryside and got out at a village. We had a cup of tea in a hut there. Apparently tourists had never been near this village so the locals didn't have the habit of begging from them and we were simply surrounded by poor villagers with terrible skins until a bus came for our return journey.

In the evening, after a hurried walk to Egmore Station with neither the time nor energy to look at shops, we caught our train and felt the luxury of having sleepers. We were actually fortunate to be in the guard's compartment, so we didn't have to watch our baggage like hawks as we had previously had to do. Although others joined us, it never became overcrowded.

On waking the following day 10th May we continued to enjoy the company of all the friendly passengers who were with us. We looked out at the countryside from the window and the tall Palmyra palm trees. One of the passengers actually bought us breakfast, and the questions they asked us were of quite a deep nature. It was good to be able to have a real exchange of views and information.

At lunch time, after an eighteen hour journey, we reached the narrow sea bridge to the Indian island of Rameshwaram. It was the strangest sensation not to be able to see any sides to the bridge as we crossed it but only water, as though we were miraculously chugging over the sea. Once on the other side, we had the feeling that our journey through India was almost complete. This was considered to be the second most sacred Hindu place to come to so there were many pilgrims, but I didn't feel any anxiety here. Perhaps the pilgrims did not come here primarily to die or be cured of their diseases as they had at Varanasi.

The humidity here was incredible. Our clothes clung to us with sticky heat, and everywhere the smell of damp was rife. We found a Lakshmi Lodge which was for pilgrims to stay the night and then went in search of something to eat. Rameshwaram was a simple, undeveloped place and we were happy to find a friendly cafe where we were able to have fried eggs with rice and dhal on a banana leaf and drink some lemon tea. There were no plates or cutlery, and we had to keep folding the banana leaf up at the edges to stop the dhal from flowing on to the table and then on to our legs! We also had a delicious desert which was like a large fritter and was served with lime juice and sugar.

The meal over, we wandered to the temple and it proved to be a very strange and interesting covered complex with arcades to walk in. Inside, there were souvenir shops, beautiful murals and ceiling paintings, though not well preserved, and intricately carved pillars, rather crudely painted in browns and yellows. We heard tribal-like drums and chanting and watched as a canopied carriage was carried by some men. Although we could not see them, inside the carriage were the ladies of the temple.

Temple gopuram in Rameshwaram

I had to face another fear. We were told that there were hook worms on the beach which could get into the body through the feet and climb up into the stomach. How safe England seemed compared with these countries that we were visiting!

Monday 11th May was a nightmare of a day. We had another look at the temple complex and watched the temple elephant dancing to the music all alone. Then we wandered down to the Indian customs office after a good breakfast. What a fiasco! We waited in various queues for about three hours to get the boat to Ceylon, and it would have been even longer if David had not complained. David said his complaining worked because the Indians did not like to be criticised and felt guilty.

The ferry was one and a half hours late in setting off. On board, there were many people, including school children and a cricket team. We spent much of the crossing talking to another traveller called Alan who had come to Asia on a spiritual quest. His goal was to lose himself through a journey of self discovery. That kind of paradox had meaning for me though I didn't always agree with how Alan told us it had to be done. He'd spent two days with an Indian mystic who had taught him that we are not always aware of the different realities, which consist of sight, sound, smell, taste, colour and wave lengths. I don't remember him mentioning touch.

The mystic then sent him on to another part of India to stay with a female abstract artist who somehow exemplified these realities in her painting. However, it seemed to me that Alan was more impressed by the fact that her husband was an important person in the police force who had made quite a fuss of him. I found it very interesting to learn what people did in their search for reality. I did notice, however, that Alan didn't have any real desire to share his discoveries when I questioned him deeply and wasn't at all interested in my thoughts about the subject, quickly squashing any ideas that I had that were different from his. David did not like him at all.

We arrived in Ceylon at Talaimannar which was located in the north western part of Mannar Island. At customs, we gave Alan $20 so he could get through. The organisational skills of the customs officials were excellent but that alone might not have been enough to get us through quickly had we not been amazingly lucky and managed by chance to join the right queue from the very beginning. We were also given preferential treatment along with the cricket team.

However, we then had to wait another five and a half hours in the train while the rest of the ferry passengers passed through customs. We could hardly keep our eyes open but sleep was impossible and there were no third class sleepers available. Once on the move, with too many people for the space, it was a difficult journey. One man insisted on having the window wide open all night and the ensuing wind on my body left me cold for once and powerless to do anything about it.

As the dawn came up the following day, my tired spirits rose a little too because I could see some incredibly green and lush tropical countryside rolling by. However, I was feeling ill: I had a sore throat, heavy head and swollen feet. I began to doze.

Occasionally, I woke up and caught sight of lily pad ponds and paddy fields, trees and palms that I'd never seen before, some with red and orange blossom. Jungle creepers wound their way through the trees, exotic birds and butterflies with jewelled colours flitted from place to place and buffaloes grazed and worked. Sometimes we passed a village of little thatched houses set amidst giant palm trees. I had always been fascinated by the plants in the huge tropical green houses in Kew Gardens but they could only give a slight hint of the overwhelming tropical beauty that we were privileged to see here.

We arrived in Colombo the capital at 12:30 a.m. on 12th May and proceeded to wait a long time for a bus. Eventually, a kind woman who was also in the queue, offered us a lift with her and her family in a taxi. She told us that she had received much kindness in England. I was glad to hear this and it was such a relief to be off our feet and going towards somewhere to sleep. They took us all the way to the youth hostel which was situated in a salubrious, tree-lined road, full of doctors and other professionals I believe. We went straight to bed and I slept for five hours then and another six hours over night which would have been even longer if we had not been woken by some loud American women.

I felt too ill and exhausted to keep up my journal for the next ten days so only wrote later. I didn't know it at the time, but it was probable that I had contracted hepatitis. I found this out when we eventually returned to England and went to the Hospital for Tropical Diseases where they found this in my blood, together with some huge worms in my stomach.

We realised that in just one week we had covered 2000 miles of which 105 hours had been spent on trains, a bus and a ferry! We had averaged four hours sleep a night. We had both lost a lot of weight and David was having trouble keeping his trousers up.

In Colombo, we were surprised to see things that we were accustomed to see in London: church spires, red double-decker buses, red pillar boxes and men who, though in local dress, were carrying large, black or colourful umbrellas to keep the heat at bay. We stayed in Colombo for longer than we wanted in order to give me a chance to recover, but the expensive cost of living there, the difficulty in getting privacy, rest or good transport and the suffocating heat made us decide that we would leave on the 17th May. I still hardly had the strength to hold up my head.

Street scene outside the Ceylon Chamber of Commerce
with an ex-London bus

The locals laughed at us a lot too and talked about us as though we weren't there. We felt as though we were animals in a zoo! One Sinhalese man who worked in the bank ran his hands over my body with no thought either of my feelings or of the fact that David was with me. I could just imagine how horrified my father who also worked in a bank would have been. We learnt later in our travels through Ceylon that we had arrived just before the general elections in which the mainly communist party was likely to take power. They were planning to ban all things western, which helped us to understand why we were meeting quite a lot of aggression.

We did spend one pleasant morning before we left Colombo bathing at Mt Lavinia beach resort, though the current was dangerous, and the monsoons had started. We also went to the cinema and saw 'One Hundred Rifles'. We were surprised to see that it was uncensored which embarrassed the locals. Half way through the showing it stopped, the lights went on and everyone with one accord leapt up and went out! There were only men in the cinema. We decided to follow them as we weren't sure what was happening, and to our amusement, discovered them all in the foyer smoking! The film resumed later.

I also enjoyed sitting quietly at the outside café of a hotel by Beira Lake sipping iced tea with lime. There was something rather magical about the lake with its green depths and monitor lizards. These large reptiles seemed like fairy tale monsters to my eyes. The view of an island at the other end with a romantic building of some sort on it added to its mystical charm. But I was beginning to feel cut off from England and home-sick. In the two and a half months since we'd left Ibiza, I had not heard from my father. Given the speed of our travels, it was actually quite possible that he had written and that we'd left any city he'd addressed a letter to before it had even arrived.

On 17th May, after posting off some letters and parcels including four reels of film to England, we left Colombo by train for Hikkaduwa on the south coast of Ceylon around midday, travelling with a companionable Sinhalese chap. He had lived in England for much of his life and had spent the last seven years in Kingston, Jamaica, having only just returned to Ceylon. He wanted to go back to England but felt his parents needed him. We felt that he had become so westernised that he might have some difficulty adapting back to life in Ceylon.

We got off the train and set off in the direction of Coral Gardens to find a hotel we'd been recommended but were stopped by a local called George who offered us his bungalow for 5 rupees a night. I felt half dead and was so comforted by the homeliness of the place. It was also very close to the most amazing beach and I thought this would be a wonderful place for me to get my health back. At nights, as we went to and fro from our bungalow through the dark palm trees, we were kept company by the tiny flashing lights of the fire flies darting around us. I slept for thirteen hours each day for several days and gradually felt my spirits returning along with my strength and health.

Hikkaduwa was a paradise and the whole area was tropically lush. It was a small fishing town in the middle of a jungle of giant coconut palm trees, the tallest perhaps sixty to seventy feet tall (18 to 21 metres,) almost all bending the same way and sighing in the breeze. The palm leaf houses, shielded from the winds by these trees, ran parallel with the narrow beach. We could walk along the shore line, through the palm trees, dipping our feet into the blue sea, often having miles of fine, golden sand to ourselves and the sand crabs. Or so we thought, until, back in England, looking at the slide David had taken of me walking on that beach in my bikini, I saw the dark figure of a man hiding behind a coconut palm. With the approaching monsoon, the sea was too rough for us to swim in or to explore the wonderful coral reef that we'd heard about.

I am watched on Hikkaduwa beach.

Fishing from the beach

Fishing from their outriggers

Once, when we were walking along the road by the beach, a car stopped and three young men offered to share their arrack with us: a very potent spirit made from the fermented sap of unopened flowers of the coconut palm. They wanted to take us with them to a place where we could have even better arrack but we decided to decline after noticing after the first sip how strong it was!

The people in this small town were for the most part uneducated and led a simple life. Many of the men were fishermen. Although some of the locals begged at times, no one was starving as they were surrounded by the bounty of nature. The only sign of progress and certainly danger were the cars and buses that sped through the roads unheeding of the ox carts. The locals had not seen many westerners if any, and we drew large crowds wherever we went. Their reaction was also to stare and laugh but there was also friendliness with it and we were beginning to get used to feeling like objects of curiosity.

One day we walked along the beach past the fishing huts to the other side of the village and stopped to rest. The crowds soon gathered and some men and boys with wiry bodies shinned up the palm trees at great speed to cut down three fresh coconuts with large knives and watch us drink the water from them and eat the transparent flesh. It drew lots of laughter from them. They also offered us small, red fruits which they clearly enjoyed but which we found rather acidic.

We had a similar experience when we stopped to rest from a walk into the interior. The crowds surrounded us at very close quarters, staring at us with their toothless grins. Someone fetched us some nuts and another brought fruit. Then the woman whom we'd seen in the garden near to where we were staying invited us into their house to take some rice and typical curried food. It was a beautifully prepared meal, ending in delicious, fresh mangoes. Even though David had no trouble getting through it all, it was more than I could manage unfortunately. It was so generous of them. One man there spoke a little English and we learnt that all the members of their extended family lived there, consisting of mother, father, brother, daughters, their husbands and children! I felt very fortunate to have access to the space I had at home.

It was the time of Vesak while we were there: the most holy day for Buddhists, commemorating the Buddha's birth, enlightenment and death. As Hikkaduwa was a small town the celebrations were not elaborate but we certainly enjoyed the atmosphere in the evening. The procession along the only street consisted of various groups of dancers including children, musicians, singers and worshippers and one highly decorated elephant. I found the Kandy style male and female dancers the most interesting, with their delicately positioned hand and feet movements. I had no idea what these meant other than that they suggested subtle expressions of meaning and they were certainly beautiful to watch. The Pandol, about thirty feet high, displaying representations of Buddha, was illuminated with flashing coloured lights.

Dancers in their finery

Children celebrating Vesak

We left Hikkaduwa on 23rd May. We could have happily stayed there much longer as it was so beautiful but we had very little time left if we were going to make it home in time for David's architectural course. It was a perfect day and hard to drag ourselves away from that blue sea and golden sand. We took the bus to Galle, near where Don, a chap we'd met on the boat, lived and where we had been invited to stay. We sat on the top deck and on one side enjoyed the views of the amazingly lush countryside where some of the palm trees had leaves so gigantic I could hardly believe it. On the other side, we caught occasional glimpses of fisherman out to sea, sitting on their stakes.

In Galle, we made for the walled city and stood on the famous grass-topped ramparts looking out to sea. We then caught a bus to Walahanduwa where Don lived. We walked the last mile to his house to the delight of the locals but unfortunately, because we had stayed longer in Hikkaduwa than we had told him we would, he was no longer there.

His parents could not speak any English but they still made us feel very welcome. His mother was a lovely old woman with the most beautiful dark eyes. His father had his hair tied in a little bun at the back of his head. His uncle was able to explain the situation to us and told us that Don had had to start a new job where he was called to travel to various sites. We shared something of our travels with them. They gave us bananas to eat and salty biscuits followed by fruit salad, and then Don's father took us back to Galle to find the bus we needed for Matara. Just as we left the house, the rains began.

Soon, we were tearing down the narrow roads again to Matara in a double-decker bus, taking the corners at ridiculous speeds, the horn blaring and the driver having no regard for the crowds in his way. People wanting the bus waved frantically at the bus stops but the driver seemed to react at a whim, refusing to stop at all sometimes or suddenly screeching to a halt some hundred yards after the stop! We never saw any sign of tourists, either on the beautiful beaches, inland or in the villages. Would it always be like this we wondered?

We found Mike, one of the three representatives whom we'd met earlier in Hikkaduwa, at the Chandra Hostel. It was full of reps and very comfortable. He treated us to a meal at the restaurant next door. We then joined him for a little arrack and then went to bed.

The following day 24th May we bought some red fish in the market which the restaurant cooked for us and we shared it with Mike. Feeling rather queasy, we eventually slept until dawn. We had hoped to swim but the monsoon proper had set in and it had rained heavily all day and night. Even so, we braved the weather to walk into town and bought maps and flip flops. We also walked round an interesting piece of modern architecture close to the beach called the Geoffrey Bawa building. David wasn't sure that it was the right design for its landscape but he was impressed by the originality of its design.

In the afternoon, Mike took us to his Catholic church. The sermons had recently been shortened from one and a half hours to half an hour, and quite honestly, I would have cut it down even more, but then I'm uncomfortable with that sort of ritual. It wasn't even a high church but most of the half hour was given to ritual or to us standing, sitting and then standing again. The most fascinating part for us was the five minute political sermon at the beginning on the importance of communist 'right' voting to save the church, themselves, their children, the country and the world!

The general elections were to be held in a few days time, which was interesting to us as England was also due to have them on 18th June before we arrived back. It was to be the first time that eighteen year olds would be allowed to vote in the U.K. We fully expected the Labour party under Harold Wilson to get in again. In the event, it was the Conservatives who were to win against the predictions of most opinion polls under the leader Edward Heath.

We'd seen and heard about the hardships, lack of freedom and education for so many people during our journey. We'd even had a taste of hardship ourselves. We'd heard about corruption in the governments of so many different countries so however much we complained about either of our main parties, we felt privileged to live in England.

We gathered that there were two political parties in Ceylon: the Unionist party which was the one currently in power, and the Coalition party which we were told was really a Communist party. The Communists were appealing to the poor, the university graduates and post-graduates as there were so few jobs for them in Ceylon just as we were told was true in the rest of Asia. Highly educated people were forced to do really menial jobs to make any living at all.

There were political meetings being held everywhere with huge, noisy crowds and they were as much entertainment as they were political, with film stars and celebrities supporting one or other party and making declamatory speeches. Accounts filled the newspapers. Education was free and I believe it was also free at university but the problem for the poor was that they couldn't let their children attend since they needed them to work. They also would never have been able to buy the necessary books or equipment, and at university, they could not have afforded meals or to rent lodgings. Currently, the university at Colombo was closed because of student riots. There had likewise been a lot of rioting at Calcutta University from those supporting the neo-communist party known as the Naxalites.

On Monday 25th May we took the early express bus for a six hour ride to Haputale up country. En route, we passed the most southerly point of our journey and followed the coast at reckless speed along narrow roads and through palm tree country as far as Hambantota where the boats were pulled up on the sands of a lovely calm blue bay. A political meeting was in progress and one man had taken advantage of the crowds to sell them aphrodisiacs!

As we turned north inland, the countryside changed and the trees were deciduous with bush and forest.

After Wellawaya as we climbed higher it grew steadily colder to 65 degrees Fahrenheit (about 18 degrees Celsius) which we found difficult to adapt to: it seemed freezing after the high temperatures we had become accustomed to. We went through a pass with a beautiful waterfall. Higher up there were rubber trees and finally the tea plantations at Haputale, about 4,700 feet above sea level. We were so disappointed that the monsoons were here also which meant low cloud as it was reputed to have one of the best views in the world.

We stayed in a very comfortable hotel that we had been recommended called the Highcliffe, owned by a friendly, elderly chap called Mr Mendis. Strangely to us, it had an English, Edwardian feel. The windows had old lead and coloured glass and all around the lounge there were reproductions of paintings by Van Gogh and old photos of hunting scenes. We stayed in the lounge all afternoon reading and playing an Asian table game like billiards with counters to the accompaniment of jazz, and for supper we had beef stew!

For breakfast, we were served by a servant with scrambled egg from a silver platter and had toast and marmalade. I had never been made to feel so important and got something of the feeling of how it must have been for the British when they settled in colonial Ceylon.

While looking through various periodicals at the hotel, I came across an American religious magazine called 'The Pentecostal Evangelical' with a priceless short letter from a woman seeking an answer to her concern. It read: 'My husband is a Christian Scientist. For years I have prayed that he might be saved. What more can I do?' I don't remember the answer now and only wish I could. I presume they ignored the inference that he needed saving from Christian Science and assumed she meant he was ill!

The next morning on 26th May we hoped to see the view, but we had climbed half way up the hill when the mists rolled in. We caught a glimpse of it though and could see that it was magnificent. We also took a walk around the factory where the tea was processed. However, because it was drawing near to Election Day, most of the workers were missing and we were shown round at great speed. I remember enough to know that two leaves and a bud were picked to make the tea. The smell of drying tea leaves pervaded the factory. They rolled it, graded it and finally purified it.

The following day 27th May we were sorry to say goodbye to Mr Mendis and his staff and the unusual comfort and security of this life but we needed to continue our journey. We got up early to have another go at climbing the hill to One Man Post and this time succeeded before the mists set in. Below us we could see an amazing panorama of lakes, the sea and a distant mountain range. It was well worth the effort. We then just managed to catch the 8.30 a.m. train to Nuwara Eliya, the highest town in Ceylon and where the British had settled. The Scottish had particularly enjoyed the cool climate there and were able to grow potatoes as well as tea. There were wonderful views all the way of the tea estates, hills and forests as we climbed high near the Horton Plain.

Once in Nuwara Eliya we caught a bus to our destination which was known as the Service Centre for the Youth Hostel Association. We had been used to the segregation of the sexes in English youth hostels but David and I were allowed to share a room. The food was excellent and inexpensive and we felt it would give us a chance to build up our physical reserves ready to face our gruelling journey overland back to England.

It was now really cold and what with the drizzle and mist, David was getting quite miserable as he had always hated that sort of weather in England. Englishness pervaded Nuwara Eliya: even the houses were mock Elizabethan and had rose gardens, dahlias, evenly mown lawns and well-tended hedges while poinsettias provided us with a reminder of where we actually were. There was a well-cut golf course too and a horse racing course. Moors ran down to a lake and there was a park which, with all its English flowers, could have been in England.

View to the south from up country

Election Day had arrived and everyone was on edge. Women had formed themselves into orderly queues outside the school polling station to vote. It was all very beautiful here but very strange. While we were wandering around, a simple fellow joined us and I found his constant mutterings quite difficult to take, but David was wonderful in the consideration and respect he showed him.

In the afternoon, we visited the Hakgala Botanical Gardens which I loved. It was another paradise but this time it had been man-made. The gardens had been informally landscaped on different levels, and as well as flowers such as delphiniums, roses, orchids and poinsettias, there were wonderful trees and shrubs. I fell in love with the fernery, which was planted amidst rock gardens and pools and I particularly enjoyed the tree ferns which I had never seen before.

While there, we met the plant labeller and were very impressed by his knowledge, his active, curious mind, his sense of fun and obvious diligence. We hoped that he would have his heart's desire and become the curator there but it seemed that for people like himself there was little opportunity for promotion. We told him as much as we could in answer to his questions about England. He surprised us by telling us that there were leopards in the gardens! We also learnt that it was said that this area was given to the demon king Ravana as a pleasure garden and when he abducted Sita, he kept her hidden here.

In the evening, we watched an old American rather paranoid science fiction film about an attack from the Chinese. I was beginning to feel quite at home! We were frozen in bed, even with all our clothes on and a blanket over us and we were unable to sleep much that night anyway because of all the celebratory fireworks and rowdy behaviour as a result of the elections.

On Thursday 28th May we set off in the drizzle to catch the morning train from Nanu Oya en-route to Darawella to watch a rugby match between the 'up country' team and the Blackheath team from London, England. There was a lot of excitement on the platforms with students shouting and marching up and down as a result of the elections and we thought at this point that the Nationalists had got back into power again and that this was a protest procession. There were similar crowds shouting and singing on the train. We got out at Hatton and waited an hour for a bus to take us to Darawella.

We eventually arrived at the rugby club towards the end of lunch time for what was to prove a fascinating time. We walked into the rather grand club and straight into the members' room. We discovered that the match was not taking place until 5 pm and so we were invited to relax in the comfort of the club. Several of the men who had come from Colombo and who were friendly, sophisticated, educated and probably wealthy, gave us the remains of their lunch. They also requested our company as their guests to the dinner and dance that was due to take place after the match.

Meanwhile, they enlightened us as to the results of the election: the Socialist / Communist Party, which was also comprised of the Ceylon Freedom Party with Mrs Bandaranaike as the leader, had got in with such a huge majority that there was virtually no opposition at all. No one knew exactly what this would ultimately lead to but it was thought-provoking to be privy to their discussion. Our new friends told us that the Party had got in by promising the poor people two free measures of rice instead of the one measure that the Nationalists had been giving them. They had also of course gained the student and post graduate vote with the promise of jobs.

It was so interesting to watch and listen as more and more wealthy people came into the club. There was clearly a British legacy here and many upper middle class British descendants who spoke in ways that were from an earlier time: extremely posh and seemingly far more English than we were ourselves. We thought that they probably owned many of the tea plantations. They were of course extremely worried about what would happen to them, their servants and their possessions with the communist party now in power. We heard such comments as,

'Look here, man, what will happen to our swimming pools?'

They were the wealthy in-crowd and they were generous with us and treated us to snacks, drinks and conversation.

We managed to procure good seats in the pavilion for three rupees each, and watched the teams go onto the beautifully kept ground. The English lads were taller and heavier but could not out do the locals in rugby attire and extremely tight trousers. In fact one of their team split his trousers completely during the course of the match! It was an enjoyable game to watch, though the up-country team was completely out-matched and seemed so loathe to tackle the Blackheath team that it was an easy win for our lads. Perhaps there was a kind of respectful inhibition about winning against an English side, but how could I know?

The Blackheath team have their photo taken

When it was over, the teams and smart crowds came into the pavilion to gossip and drink. Many of the women were elegant with their elaborate hairdos and short dresses. They could have been half English or Dutch and some of them had probably come out with the team from England. I began to feel really uncomfortable and unattractive in my much worn Asian attire and my unwashed hair, and even David felt uncomfortable in his shorts. I had just washed his Indian trousers, so we tried not to stand out which of course had the effect on us of feeling left out because no one came near us!

Eventually, David's trousers were dry and he went off to change. While I was thinking how lucky I was to be in this interesting situation, the tea estate manager we'd been introduced to earlier, Arthur, who also owned a rubber plantation came and joined me with a drink. Then another of the men we had talked to earlier, Pradeep, also joined us and apologised for ignoring us and explained that he and his friend were the chief pickers of the teams that were playing the two test matches against Blackheath.

David rejoined us and we chatted with Arthur who invited us to stay the night with him. We were delighted because we had been wondering what we were going to do about getting back to the Service Station after the dance. By this time, everyone was beginning to get very drunk, including us. David had started with beer and was now on whiskey. I was drinking gin and orange, and the measures were huge.

David decided to go and speak to the Blackheath team while I talked to Pradeep. We were discussing politics and society when he suddenly asked me what my religion was. Normally, after such a question, I would have answered simply that it was Christianity but for some reason, I decided to tell him that it was Christian Science.

He wanted to know all about it. Well that was a tall order and I didn't know why I chose the specific aspect I decided on at that moment. I said that when Christ had been crucified and was about to pass on from this life he had told his disciples not to worry, that he would come again. About one hundred years ago, a woman called Mary Baker Eddie had discovered Christian Science through a revelation direct from God. Christian Science was the Christ made universal, showing that all men were in fact Christ if they understood the Science of Being. At this point we were interrupted but he was very excited by what I had told him and said that he was already converted. He wanted us to come to dinner with him once we returned to Colombo for me to tell him more about it.

I was happy at this prospect because it was so rare for me to tell anyone that I was a Christian Scientist, even close friends as I felt that most people would find it too unusual and complicated to say the least. Meanwhile, David came back with Ravi, a young tea planter who had a tea estate in Nuwara Eliya and who wished we had met him before so that we could have stayed with him. He had a very dark complexion, long hair and unusual accent. He promised to send us some of his tea when we were back in England. He couldn't do enough for us, wanting to buy us everything in sight and obviously encouraged by the amount he'd had to drink! By now, we had received six tickets for dinner!

David continued talking to Ravi but I got up and found myself in the same corner of the room as one of the large Blackheath team members, Andrew. We got into conversation and hit it off immediately. I enjoyed his attentiveness and sensitivity. Then Ravi asked me to dance, and he got much too close for comfort. He kept squeezing my hand and repeating that he wished we'd met him before. I excused myself but he caught up with me later and we danced again. Luckily Andrew came in and asked him if he could dance with me. Ravi agreed and we found that we both enjoyed dancing in the same abandoned way. It was wonderful release of feelings to dance in this way after so long.

Eventually, we had dinner which really wasn't very good, and after that, I spent most of the time dancing with different people. The band was adequate but unfortunately, David and I weren't able to dance together as he was looking after our bag. I don't think he minded much actually as he was sozzled and sleepy.

Finally, at about 1 a.m., Arthur decided to leave. Andrew kissed me and asked me to come to their final match at the club. Arthur drove us back to his place in his new jeep with the servant in the back who we discovered had been guarding the jeep all evening.

What a life! It was a seven mile drive past the two tea factories he managed to his large bungalow and garden. He stopped at one of the factories where wheels were still busily turning, and spoke to the watchman there. I was rather shocked at his tone. He mentioned what was happening the following day when an important visitor was due to visit the factory and said to him,

'Make some good tea, man, because you know what I'll do to you if you don't, don't you!'

I wasn't sure how serious he was but the watchman seemed to think so as he kept backing away from him.

Once ensconced in the bungalow, we sat in his lounge and Arthur insisted that we have another drink. It seemed that he needed someone to talk to for he was a lonely man. Six weeks earlier, his wife had walked out on him and left him with the three children. Neither he nor his wife had since got in touch with the other and he told us that he didn't have much hope in them getting back together as they were each as stubborn as the other. It was very sad but we were so tired by now and it was difficult to give him the attention he required. Meanwhile, it was interesting to see something of how he lived. He put his feet up, patted his Alsatian dog and ordered his servants about. He was rather bitter about the last of the 'bl---y colonials: stuck up bu--ers, all of them!'

He was also extremely nervous about the outcome of the elections. He had recently bought 300 acres of rubber plantation which he hoped to divide between his sons and son-in-law. Apart from the worry of what might happen to all that he owned, he had been politically active against the Communist party, speaking publically against them and he feared he might well end up in prison.

Finally, we managed to disengage ourselves to go to bed and had a wonderfully comfortable sleep. We should have been happy not to have been woken up early but Arthur had to be off at 7:30

a.m. and apparently that time was considered late by Sinhalese standards. He came to say goodbye while we were still in bed. We discovered the reason for his stopping at one of the factories the night before: apparently the owner was making his quarter yearly visit, and it was giving him yet another reason to worry about his future.

It was now 29ᵗʰ May and David and I started the day in comfort with each of us having our own man servant to serve us breakfast in a room overlooking the beautiful garden. We had scrambled eggs, dhal and string hoppers, which were spirals of flat, rice noodles, and bananas with a large pot of tea. Then one of the servants whisked us away and drove us to Talawakele station in an old Standard car to await the Kandy train. We were rather sad to leave since the house was so comfortable, the garden a mass of colour, and I should have liked to have had the opportunity to cheer Arthur up.

On our journey to the station, the views were wonderful, and we were delighted to pass the Devon Estate and a waterfall called Devon Falls and wondered what the link was with that county in England, especially as David had grown up there. He managed to get a shot of it, including Arthur's estate and home in the background. We also passed another lovely waterfall called Clair Falls.

We caught a crowded train to Kandy and went the last part of the way in an overcrowded bus which was as usual driven recklessly: we had to hold on to the seat in front to make sure that we weren't shaken to the floor. A lucky accident though took us past a shoe shop where a young chap I had met the night before worked. He had told us that when we arrived and found his shop, he would happily give us a lift to the Odeon which happened to be by the Y.H.A. place where we hoped to stay.

Our lift to the Odeon secured, we saw to our amusement that the film 'Far From the Madding Crowd' was on and was just about to start. We had been chasing this film all over the world, always missing it for one reason or another, and here it was in this most British of Asian countries! We took our seats immediately and thoroughly enjoyed the film: it was beautifully acted, directed and photographed, and very moving; well worth the chase.

We discovered that the Y.H.A. had been closed down so we were directed to the Boy Scouts Headquarters instead. It was only just passable, being bare and dirty, but it was only four rupees a night and we were delighted to find a good restaurant nearby called The Silverdale.

The next morning Saturday 30th May was a fine day and we were back in the warmth. We breakfasted on sweet bread and bananas, got some lunch to take away with us, then set off for the Royal Peradeniya Botanical Gardens. These were reputedly even more famous than the ones we had already visited in Ceylon. They were indeed amazing. They were vast for a start, with 147 acres of land, bounded on three sides by the Mahaweli River.

I had always been fascinated by trees as I loved the fact that they reached to the sky and yet were so grounded by their roots. That struck me as a wonderful symbol for man who sought to connect his physical life with his spirit. The essence of trees had always seemed to speak to me simply through their presence, and there were so many here from all over the world that I had never seen. Many of them were quite extraordinary in both beauty and strangeness. My suggestion for the human equivalents were the characters in a film directed by Fellini: the director who I felt chose actors who were always beautiful in spite of being flawed.

Some trees had weird fruits and leaves, trunks the colour of rainbows, and there were palms, giant creepers and huge bamboos.

One tree that had me riveted had roots coming down from each branch, and by that means it was taking possession of the ground. Perhaps it would take over the whole of the gardens! I wasn't sure of its name but we thought it was the Banyan tree. I called it 'earth-bound tree'.

Banyan tree

Another spectacular tree had a tangle of roots that looked like live snakes writhing together. Yet another had trunks so smooth that they could have been polished by human hand and they contained vast holes in them as large as separate rooms. In the greenhouses there were exotic orchids, mostly growing out of tree trunks and the gardens were teeming with wild life: exotic butterflies, chameleons, unusual birds and a profusion of squirrels. There were no doubt also other reptiles and various wild cats and other mammals but they kept out of our way.

On our return to our 'cell' in the Boy Scouts Headquarters later in the afternoon, we fell asleep immediately from exhaustion. We awoke in the evening to find it raining hard but we braved it nonetheless and arrived later at the library, dripping with water and then went on to the restaurant.

On Sunday 31st May we got up early and went to see the Buddhist Temple of the Sacred Tooth located in the Royal Palace Complex in Kandy. It was believed that whoever held the sacred tooth also held power. The tooth was also thought to have healing powers and formed the basis of rituals there by the monks. We did not manage to time our visit with any of the rituals but I found the environment of the complex with its mysterious green lake fascinating.

We went into Laksala and found a pretty batik wall hanging as a present to the Iranian family who had put us up. I also found just the kind of silver ankle bracelet I was looking for, but the women of Ceylon were much more delicate in build than I was so disappointingly I couldn't get it round my ankle.

We returned to the lake and started to walk around it. We hadn't gone far before we were amazed to see a giant monitor lizard swimming there, six or seven feet long. We didn't know what it was at the time and it seemed like some amphibious monster. It had a small head for the size of its body and a very long tongue which it flicked in and out. Unfortunately, David did not manage to photograph it but we did see several of them later.

We then made our way to the Buddhist Publication Centre as I wanted some pamphlets on Buddhism. Here, we met an interesting Dutch man. He had originally been a Catholic priest but someone had stirred up old childhood doubts in his mind about the existence of God so he had left his priesthood behind thirty five years ago and had come to live in Ceylon. For the first nine years here, he had been happy to be a Buddhist monk because there is no God in Buddhism.

However, as he began to question Buddhism and to intellectualise it, he decided to leave the monastery and begin his own version of Buddhism. He gave regular broadcasts and wrote pamphlets and books on it, and we came away with some of them to think about. He had an incredible sense of humour and much kindness but we did not seem to agree with many of his ideas really. There was one point I did agree on, however, and that was his main maxim: to have an attitude of allowing or letting, which was also the thinking resulting from the use of LSD according to its proponents.

We then caught a bus to Anuradhapura though were delayed in getting there because the usual careless driving caused a poor cyclist to get knocked down just outside of Matele. During our wait however, we met our Kandy school teacher friend, Raja, and got into conversation with him. Unbelievably, the driver was no less reckless for the rest of the journey to Anuradhapura and it was late when we arrived. We were misdirected to the hotel at Jaffna Junction and then told that it could be a trouble spot with the post election fever. This chap insisted on accompanying us to the hotel saying that it was dangerous for us to be alone! Luckily, the friendly manager was waiting at the door for us and he gave us a good meal before we slept.

The following day 1st June, after a good breakfast, we set off to explore part of the ancient religious city of Anuradhapura. It was suggested to us that we should hire bicycles to see these sacred ruins which cover over sixteen square miles and we decided to share one between us, David doing the pedalling. We'd hardly started out before we discovered we had a puncture and the men reappeared so readily to mend it that I had the feeling it was planned! They only charged us 50 cents and I reasoned they did need to earn a living somehow.

It was fascinating to see all these ruins of palaces, monasteries and monuments set out amidst lakes and countryside in the midst of a jungle. I enjoyed the day enormously. I think my favourite place though was the elegant baths with tiny terrapins swimming in them. I knew that many people would have been frustrated to see such an interesting place without a guide and I would certainly have enjoyed having one. However, I suppose it showed me that I was often more interested in atmosphere and nature than in historical facts. It got my imagination going.

We arrived back at the hotel to find wild boar on the menu, though we had been told previously of the danger of eating it as they can harbour tape worms. However, we felt that they were trying to give us a good experience during this stay and that it would be rude to decline it so we decided to go ahead and accept. Besides, it was the only food on offer! It was delicious. The manager told us that his wife lived in Colombo and they saw each other once a month or so. We thought he was probably something of a 'bon viveur', enjoying the company of other women and also, from his great size, a lot of good food! We spent a short, noisy and sleepless night in the heat.

We left for Colombo again at the ridiculously early hour of 3:30 a.m. on 2nd June travelling through the paddy fields. David got a great shot of farmers washing both buffaloes and onions.

From 3rd to 6th June, apart from planning to do some relaxing things, we also had various bits of business to sort out. We went to the post office to see if there was any mail for us and to post ours. I was happy to find a letter from my father and three from my grandmother, all of which we should have missed if we had left Ceylon earlier as planned. I was sad to see that neither of them seemed very happy with life; and yet my father had out of the blue, spent a week sailing and for the first time since his days in the Royal Navy Voluntary Reserve during the Second World War, he had seen his 'Number Two', as he referred to him.

After the post office, we went on to the British High Commission to pick up our bag. We decided not to stay in the hostel where we'd been so uncomfortable before and found the Dehiwela International Youth Hostel with fans in our room this time and easy access to the buses. Then we charged off to the cinema to see 'The Prime of Miss Jean Brodie'. We enjoyed it very much and Maggie Smith was excellent and deserved her Academy award for best actress but I thought the film was more like a stage play in its theatricality.

While in Colombo, we enjoyed an interesting few hours at the zoo and I was rather glad that I hadn't known of all the deadly snakes that were indigenous to Ceylon while we wandered around the countryside in our usual naive way! There were boas, pythons, cobras and vipers to name but a few but I found the green flying snakes that slithered vertically up the tree trunks in their camouflaged way, then 'flew' from the trees on to their preys particularly alarming.

We managed to get to the final match for Blackheath and also spent an enjoyable day with some friends we made there. We had intended to leave Colombo on the evening of 4th June but there was some unexplained crisis which meant we couldn't go.

During the course of our stay in Colombo, David and I had been eating a meal in a restaurant when we were involved in something of a drama. A young Sinhalese chap had joined us and drawn us into conversation. I found his behaviour very suspicious from the outset but was intrigued. He told us that he happened to be meeting a friend for a drink and would we like to join them.

We did so and had quite an interesting conversation with them, but all the time, I kept feeling that there was something phoney about them. They didn't seem like friends of each other for one thing and I told the young man we'd met first that they didn't seem to have a lot in common. I was also uneasy about the fact that this young chap had talked quite obsessionally to me about how selfish women were and how he had been betrayed by one particular woman.

The older man made a great thing of showing us his membership card to an elite club with his name on it. They wanted us to go to his coconut estate ten miles away. David told them that we wouldn't do this so they drove us to our hostel but the young man would not stop from trying to persuade us to go to the estate. In view of his feelings about women, I was in no mind to do this. We were not surprised when they made us a proposition; it had been coming all evening. Would we smuggle £1300 to England in return for 10% commission? We said we would think about it and I was very relieved to get out of the car. We were due to meet them again at a restaurant the following day with our decision.

When we got back to our room, we talked it over into the early hours, discussing all the aspects of their story that didn't add up. But I'm afraid that we were also somewhat tempted by the money because it might mean that we would actually be able to fly part of the way back to England instead of facing what promised to be a gruelling journey overland. We were also not the healthy people we had been when we first set out on this journey from Ibiza. We did, however, sense the danger of taking this on. We couldn't be sure that the package contained money for a start. It could be precious stones or even drugs. With the chance of being discovered at the border and ending up in some prison thousands of miles from home, it was a terrible risk. I was so relieved when at 3 a.m. David suddenly announced that we would not do it.

We told our friends about this situation the following day. They told us that this man lived near to them though they didn't know much about him except that he was very wealthy. I wondered about all this afterwards and how the chain of events might have rolled out; whether they did in fact know them well or if not whether they had decided to get the matter investigated. We would never know.

Eventually, we had to leave at short notice on 7th June, cancelling dinner out with our two friends. Instead, they took us to the station to catch the 7:15 p.m. Jaffna Mail train. We were both too exhausted to face the ferry again and had made the decision to fly to Southern India. We spent a sleepless night on the train and then had a very long walk to the airways office, only to find that we had missed the airport bus by ten minutes. However, we caught a taxi and went through customs without any bother, catching the morning plane to Madras.

On Monday at 9:45 a.m. on 8th June we touched down at Madras airport after a smooth fifty minute flight and were given preferential treatment at Madras customs and driven to the bus station. As so often had happened on this journey, we got the last two seats, this one in the Madras Express Bus leaving five minutes later. We then roared through the flat land to Madras. Although it was not actually raining, it was cloudy and not too hot, and we felt relieved to know that the hotel we were going to was comfortable because we had stayed there before.

On the bus we met a young man who was a representative for Massey-Ferguson Implements. He told us that he had been offered the choice of three wives but would probably accept his father's preferred choice. He also told us of a good store where we could buy some saris to take back called the Eastern Stores. On arriving in town, we were grateful that there was a little rain to cool the 98 degrees Fahrenheit heat (about 37 degrees Celsius). We were amazed how little we had seen previously of the shopping and commercial area of the city and were particularly interested in Mount Road where most of the trading went on.

On Tuesday morning 9th June, getting reservations with concessions for the Bombay Mail kept us busy until lunchtime. After eating again at Central Station we made our way to Eastern Stores, where we arranged for some clothes to be made up for us. I had a pair of loose trousers and a top, and we ordered a shirt for David and one for my brother Richard, all of which we would collect the following day. We also bought two lovely handloom cotton saris for me which only cost 30 rupees. During the night, I found it difficult to sleep because I was considering buying some more saris to sell in Teheran to help with our journey home. I put this to David the following morning and he agreed.

First, we had to sort out our journey to Karachi so went to the port area but could find nothing out about sailing there. We had no better luck finding any silver jewellery for me either. It was too hot to shop in that heat, - somewhere between 95 and 100 degrees Fahrenheit - so we returned to Central Station to book tickets for Bombay. Unfortunately, we had to choose between waiting ten days to travel there third class or reserve a first class compartment on a train leaving that night. Because of how tired we were we decided on the latter but it meant using up our funds worryingly fast.

Having made this decision, however, we were allowed to use the station's best facilities for a meal and to take a shower. It gives you an idea of how I was feeling at the time if I tell you that this was one of the most wonderful experiences of my life. Once in the miraculous spaciousness and under the cool, free-flowing water of this shower, I was so excited that I began to sing aloud and didn't want to come out. I think I could have stayed there forever had not an impatient traveller eventually humbled me into leaving it!

After leaving the station, we saw a pitiful sight near the bus stop opposite: a body partially covered by the live but very ill body of a beggar. It was still there in the evening and had turned a horrible colour. The heat hadn't helped and the flies were gathering. We wondered how long it would lie there as no one seemed to take responsibility for it in any way. What tragically hard lives the poor of India faced and how public their misery! Busy people were hurrying by, holding their noses or putting a handkerchief over the lower part of their faces. And yet we liked Madras. It had a very easy-going atmosphere. People accepted us, they smiled a lot and they seemed to have come to terms with this public death and misery as part of the total way of life. We noticed that we had become more accepting and objective ourselves just in the short while we had been there.

We returned to the hostel to pack and left a deposit with them. Then we cashed in all our remaining dollars and headed back to Eastern Stores to buy some more saris. Once the proprietor understood that we intended to buy quite a few, we were treated to drinks and made a fuss of which was enjoyable. It was also great fun to sit there looking through so many different saris and to spend some money for a change. Ultimately, we bought five more.

We left with heavy packages but with the prospect of doing some good business in Teheran. We picked up our bag from the hostel and paid up. We were so looking forward to our first class compartment on the Bombay Mail. The journey was going to last for two nights and a day. The train did indeed live up to our expectations with very comfortable beds, two working fans and an attendant and a shower just down the corridor. And no one to pester us!

We arrived in Bombay early in the morning of Friday 12th June to find that the monsoons were in full force. We made our way to the Taj Hotel which some kind friends had recommended as having some cheap hostel-type lodging there. We sloshed about in the wet, stepping over the waking bodies of the many poor folk who slept on the pavements. Once there, we decided it was too expensive and found a cheaper option called the Red Shield which charged 12.50 rupees per day inclusive of meals. The food was uninteresting though and not Indian. For instance, lunch was cold meat, boiled potatoes and salad. At 10 a.m. we were taken to our dormitories.

Churchill Chambers in Bombay taken from the Red Shield showing pavement sleepers

We had lots of business to see to and spent the whole morning getting soaked as we went from one place to another in the relentless deluge. I was absolutely delighted though to find the sort of delicate silver rings I had been searching for and which were inexpensive. I bought six different designs for 25 rupees in all.

We discovered that the ship to Karachi had just left and the next one would not be sailing until 24th June. After much discussion, taking into account how exhausted we were now and knowing that we had to face an incredibly demanding journey back to England overland from Karachi, we eventually decided to take a plane.

We got up early on Saturday 13ᵗʰ June and caught a taxi to the BOAC Terminal. Things went pretty well for us going through customs except that we had excess baggage. Soon, an old lady kindly persuaded her niece to organise it all for us. We had a smooth one hour twenty three minute flight in a Trident aeroplane flying out of the rain into the humid heat of Karachi. However, the minute we arrived at customs in Karachi airport, we unsuspectingly found ourselves in great trouble.

The officials were clearly expecting to find drugs on us, and presumably hoped then to gain promotion or reward. Or perhaps they thought they could bribe us. They took our carefully-packed bags apart with no regard for our belongings, throwing things around and emptying out the contents of any bottles with liquid, including all our shampoo and conditioner.

Failing to find any drugs, they came at us with another possible way in which we might have broken the law. They said that it was illegal to return to Pakistan with any money from our previous visit there. Well of course we had got some money left over, and the officials talked a lot amongst themselves about us in Urdu while we waited nervously. By now, although we were angry at this treatment, my heart was also in my mouth. Were we going to end up in a Pakistani prison after all this? I felt we'd never survive it in the run-down state we were now in.

Suddenly, we remembered that the one address Maggie had given us in Ibiza which we could use while travelling East happened to be in Karachi. We wondered if the names on this address would carry any weight with these officials as, apart from them being friends of Maggie's, we had no idea who these people were and what sort of position they had in the society here or even whether it would make any difference anyway.

David managed to find the piece of paper on which was written their names and address and told the customs officials that we were going there. After more discussion, they turned back to us, returned our piece of paper, and with the rage of disappointment and failure, told us to hurry up and pack up our bags. This was no easy task and they were belligerent now in their impatience to get rid of us.

Eventually, we managed to pack our things in some kind of jumbled order and left the officials with huge relief. We had no idea that our troubles were far from over. We made our way quickly out of the terminal to the waiting taxis which were old cars. All the drivers immediately surrounded us, hassling us to take their cab. After the comparative freedom of India, we had forgotten just how different the men in Pakistan could be. We were just about to get into one cab when we were told that we had to get into a different one.

We noticed that there was already a man sitting in the passenger seat in the front, and by now, we should have recognised that as a sign that we might not be safe. But we were in such a state of misguided relief from having escaped the customs officials that we overrode our intuition.

We put our baggage into the open boot and got into the back of the cab. Even though we had not been in touch with Maggie's friends, after all the trouble we'd been through we decided to give the driver their address which we hoped might provide us with some protection. However, as soon as we got going, we were aware that the man in the passenger seat was constantly turning round and looking past us through the rear window and whispering to the driver. We couldn't think why he should be doing this and felt very uneasy. I looked around to see what he might be looking for but could see nothing out of the ordinary.

We hadn't gone more than a mile before the cab came to a halt and the driver told us that he did not go any further. Suddenly, we were aware that another taxi had pulled up beside us. The two men from our cab leapt out and one went to get our luggage. We quickly tried to get out but found ourselves locked in! I was paralysed with fear but David dived over the front seat and out of the driver's door, racing to get our luggage which he snatched back as they were loading it into the other taxi. Thank God for his quick thinking!

There was a certain amount of talking and then the first cab drove off. There was nothing for it but to bargain with this second driver as there was no other way of travelling on. We asked him to take us to the address of Pat and Hasan and he agreed to do it for 6 rupees. It was a huge relief to us after all this. We arrived at their house and explained briefly what had happened and why we were there. We were overjoyed to find that they invited us in even though they didn't know us.

After telling them what had happened to us from when we had arrived in Karachi, we were shocked to learn that we had narrowly escaped losing our lives. Hasan told us that many travellers such as us were taken into the desert and killed for whatever luggage and money they were carrying with them. It seemed unbelievable that we had been given that one address which we'd carried on a bit of paper for thousands of miles and it was that which had saved our lives! I could have cried with gratitude and relief.

Pat and Hasan kindly invited us to stay with them. To add to the surrealism of the day, they told us that they were going to a party that night and invited us to join them, which we did. It was a farewell party for a friend who was leaving the drama club of which Hasan was also a member. We met some friendly people, ate some great food and had rather a lot to drink. We returned rather the worse for wear at 3 a.m..

We awoke late on Sunday 14th June feeling rather hung over and enjoyed a good breakfast. Just before noon, we set off by car for the coast a few miles away. The suburbs were a tight mass of concrete blocks in the cubist style with flat roofs. We saw no old houses and nothing with any character. It all seemed nondescript and rather dirty. It was a hot 95 degrees and 80% humidity so our clothes clung to us and our skin was permanently damp and sticky. We stuck to every seat we sat on!

Karachi was a dusty city which, although so humid, had very little rainfall. The year before it had only had two days of rain and the previous year, just half an hour! The sky though was full of towering masses of ominous, black clouds but they just hung there taunting everyone with promises that never materialised. David and I braved the sea and it was a delight to feel the cool of the water on our bodies but the waves were incredibly strong because of the monsoon winds. David found the battle to stay upright invigorating, but for me, it was a risky struggle not to get knocked over and dragged out to sea, and after one such near event, I conceded that I was no match for these waves and got out. To my surprise, Pat was fearless.

Back on the beach, we enjoyed a picnic of eggs, tomatoes and bread followed by mangoes to finish. The mango season was at its height and those mangoes were the best we had ever tasted. Looking around, I saw people having camel rides on the beach, Muslim girls bathing fully dressed, embassy staff enjoying a relaxing Sunday and dark skinned fishermen from the village surfing. One of them had a huge physique and long hair.

We returned to their home and dressed to go and investigate the possibility of obtaining last minute seats for a performance by the world famous French mime artist, Marcel Marceau. It was someone I had always wanted to see and would never have thought that I would realise my dream in Karachi. There were in fact no seats left, but Hasan was able to pull some strings and we were allowed to sit on the side steps for the first half and on seats during the second half. The performance featured his famous creation, Bip, - a sad, white-faced clown in a striped jumper and a battered silk opera hat. He was unforgettable. Afterwards, we ate chicken kebabs and drank lassi.

On the morning of the 15th June we went to the Iranian Embassy to sort out our visa for the return trip. We hardly liked to contemplate our homeward journey, knowing that we had to face crossing the Pakistani Desert first with little or no energy. The temperature was now 98 degrees and the humidity 74%. We spent the afternoon and evening on a leisurely trip out to sea on the 'Bunderboat' enjoying the breeze and eating asparagus sandwiches and apricots. We noticed a Russian ship and submarine in the harbour.

Pat and Hasan told us that the servants were a problem here, particularly the cooks, who wanted everything on their terms. They had dismissed their last one and had just managed to find a new one who was due to start work with them soon. Apparently, it was not acceptable for comfortably off people to do their own cooking, so life without one was seen as unbearable. Such families also usually had a 'bearer' who tended to live in and who saw to all the general chores such as laying the table and ironing the clothes and so on. However, bearers did not do anything that was considered menial such as the various cleaning jobs. For these tasks, there was the sweeper.

Monday 16th to Wednesday 24th June was a blur of anxiety and fear, and we made no entries in our journals. David awoke feeling ill. His stomach was upset and he was unable to eat a thing even though the idea of the steak and jacket potatoes on offer was so tempting. He was no better the following two days. Eventually,

Hasan called a doctor who took some of David's blood and sent it to a laboratory. The results showed that he had hepatitis. I just didn't know what to do. David was too ill to think clearly. We didn't have the money we needed to cope with this crisis and also we had heard that to be admitted into hospital, patients shared beds with each other. What else might he catch there?

The doctor said that he would arrange for a daily transfusion of dextrose, which was thought to provide the missing energy. He came every day for about ten days until David's arm began to look like a pin cushion and the doctor gradually ran out of a place to put the needle. I stayed in the bedroom with David and one day, when the doctor put the needle into David's arm, blood spurted all over the wall. I couldn't stop myself from letting out a scream! The doctor immediately said that I had been making him nervous and it was my fault this had happened.

I don't remember what happened after that. We decided that there was no chance of us being able to travel overland with David in this state. There was nothing for it but to send a telegram to my father and hope that he would agree to transfer the money we needed to buy a plane ticket back to England. I knew that he wouldn't be happy about this as he had never wanted us to go on this trip in the beginning. However, he did acquiesce and we were able to book a flight on an EL AL Airlines plane for 25th June.

It seemed that our journey had become more and more dangerous in proportion to our health and energy leaking away. And yet at each dangerous or potentially dangerous turn, we had found support. We realised that we had been incredibly lucky to have been with this couple at this time: not just because it had saved our lives when we arrived in Karachi, but also because we had received their help and the comfort of their home in this crisis. It seemed that the party with all that alcohol had been the catalyst for David's hepatitis to come out. I realised with huge gratitude that we could so easily have missed that party by one day, in which case we might have been in the middle of the Pakistani desert when he became ill; without friends, comfort, civilisation or the means to communicate with the outside world.

We said goodbye to Hasan and Pat and caught the Super-Caravelle at 12:10 a.m. Pakistani time on Thursday 25th June, making our first stop at Sharjah in Iran. In Doha, Qatar, we stopped for half an hour for the plane to refuel and were approached by a Jordanian with $4,000 for us if we would meet him at a hotel in Damascus. God knows what he wanted of us!

We had a two hour wait and change of plane at Damascus. We learnt that there had indeed been heavy fighting along the Israeli / Syrian border since we had left Damascus: the heaviest since the five day war. In fact, the week before, a plane had been shot down. England was still a long way away.

Once up in the sky, we looked down over Beirut and the Lebanese mountains and were soon taking breakfast overlooking a brown, sun-baked Cyprus, then Rhodes and the various Greek islands until we landed at Athens with its clear, blue sea. The weather was quite beautiful here with an ideal temperature in contrast to all those extremes that we had experienced for the last four months or so. We stayed here for half an hour.

Once the plane had refuelled, we continued our journey homeward, eventually flying down over the flat, green, rolling countryside of what was then known as Czechoslovakia to land at Prague. We were not surprised to see that the planes in the airport were mainly Russian. In 1968, that year of political unrest in so many countries, Alexander Dubcek, briefly president of Czechoslovakia, had tried to establish 'socialism with a human face'. The Russians had reacted with tanks and troops. When we landed there, we saw many young people watching from the roof of the airport, prisoners in their own land. Once we were all inside the airport building, we found ourselves locked in too until the plane had refuelled yet again and then we were all marched back to the plane with an armed guard.

Le Bourget in France was covered in a dense, cloud which seemed to reflect something of my own state of mind.

After a journey of about 22 hours, what a mixture of feelings I had as we touched down at Heathrow at 4 pm the following day 26th June: huge relief to be in a safer, more civilised part of the world after so long living with daily uncertainties, discomforts and frequent dangers; jet lag, exhaustion and confusion from travelling such distances for so long and having to process so many varied experiences; and some anxiety about getting David home. We had yet to face customs and then the Underground before reaching my father's house in Ealing, and I wasn't sure that David would be able to remain on his feet for that long.

Surprisingly, the customs officials gave us no trouble getting through and then somehow, in a disconnected daze, we found enough adrenalin to cope with this concluding stage of our marathon journey: the Underground to Acton Town station and then a final taxi back to my father's house. I had been away from England for nearly a year. In that time, David had only made a brief visit back there. We had left Ibiza on 1st March and had been travelling for about four months. Our thin, weak bodies were a testimony to the trials of this journey, our minds and emotions over-stimulated. However, we had certainly had an adventure and we had succeeded in coming home.

Conclusion

It strikes me that there is a sense in which our consciousness is our true home and we carry this with us wherever we go. This particular journey spoke of my own consciousness and was a different experience for David even though we travelled together. It was also unique in the sense in which that time and those places no longer exist in the way that they did when we travelled. Knowing that our own experiences also impact others, so often in ways that we are unaware of, I have sometimes wondered what sort of trail we left behind us.

It was certainly an adventure and I rather think that we are all here to have our own adventure. In fact, we probably discover most about ourselves either when we are pushed or when we choose to step out of our comfort zone.

For me, it was a journey within a journey. As I wrote this account, I could certainly see how it was part of my own much longer journey to become grounded and more connected to my emotions. I had been given two warnings of this in Ibiza. Within a year of returning home, I had a breakdown. That was the beginning for me of a huge journey of a very different nature to discover a new, more integrated way of being that would reconcile my spiritual awareness with how I experienced life. That journey has taken me the rest of my life and is the subject of another book.

Epilogue 2015

I t was an amazing privilege for us to be able to take this journey and at this time before technology and easy communication made the world and its different events instantly known and defined through the eyes of others. Reporting, with the tendency to see mainly bad events as newsworthy, has created narrow collective beliefs and fears. When openness and trust have closed down, our world can become a frightening place.

The experience that David and I had in each country we travelled through reflected back to us our belief that people for the most part were kind, generous and accepting of us; also that people of different religions, countries and backgrounds could live together harmoniously. Yes, we were naive and idealistic but it has continued to be our experience since then that maintaining an open-hearted curiosity and trust in people tends to bring out the best in them.

In spite of and perhaps because of the extreme changes taking place in the world, it is more than ever an exciting time to be alive now. The inspiration of the 1960s and 70s that led so many of us to believe that we could change the world by changing ourselves never died. The former counterculture and influence of Eastern thought in the 1960s evolved in the 1970s into what came to be known as the New Age Movement in the West. It has been gathering momentum exponentially to this day, quietly and powerfully finding its outlet through many paths.

Essentially, it is a spiritual movement with a holistic view of reality. It recognises the connection of all things and the need for each of us to take care of our whole being. It leans on intuitive wisdom rather than information gathering with an emphasis on personal growth, healing and transformation.

Likewise, the sciences have evolved, and increasingly are finding evidence to back this paradigm shift in consciousness. In fact, the technologies, resources and knowledge for all of us to live quality lives in freedom together already exist. It simply demands of us a willingness to adapt and open to a new way of being.

Forty five years on from our journey, many of the places we visited in the Middle East and Asia are increasingly fragmented, and as I write this, there is little indication of peace. Positions between some of these countries are more entrenched, and conflict has become more complex: different factions seek power, some extending into many parts of the world, and major powers vie for control.

Millions of refugees are on the move, taking perilous journeys to seek safety elsewhere. Such a huge crisis demands cooperation between nations on an unprecedented scale and a response that is holistic, compassionate and wise. It seems that world events are demanding of nations what life demands of us individually: that we must adapt and grow and discover depths of kindness and creative solutions together for the good of the whole world.

In spite of how dark the world can appear, I am convinced that every human being has a place of wisdom and love inside themselves. This light may lie dormant, or insignificant like a candle in the dark, but all the darkness in the world can never put out that light.